Shorter and Sweeter

As You Like It

By

Shandra Love

Edited by Courtney L. Smith

Shorter and Sweeter

As You Like It

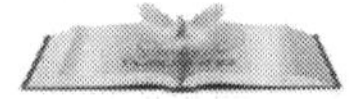

Spiritscribe Publishing, LLC
P.O. Box 2241
Humble, Texas 77347
www.spiritscribepublishing.com
(832) 445-6229

ISBN 978-0-578-47303-1

Acknowledgments

To the many family members, friends, and dedicated readers who continue to allow me into your world long enough to deliver more of my literary accomplishments. Your support, encouragement, and feedback are what inspire me to keep doing what I do best. “Thank you” multiplied by infinity.

Shandra*

Table of Contents

My Soldier

I jumped up and rushed to the restroom to run bath water.

"Oh shoot! I can't believe I overslept like that!" I said aloud as I hurried through the house, gathering my thoughts with the articles of clothing I will be wearing when I go pick Ken up from the airport. He would be here today, and I could not wait. We have longed to be with each other for months, now. We met online. The phone calls and love letters had been great, but actually seeing him would be the pleasure principle.

It started out so sweet and unsuspecting. We met on one website (when we signed one another's guest logs), and, as time went on, we learned we had another site in common. We would exchange information and slowly begin to experience a love that was so sweet, nurturing, and deep. Being together was all we desired.

He was in a foreign land, serving the United States as a soldier in the Army. He had been there since the attack on the World Trade Center, and he was ready to be back on American soil.

The alarm clock went off, and I almost jumped out of my skin. I looked around somewhat dazed and confused at how I got back in bed. When I looked at the clock, I realized I had been dreaming. I let out a laugh of relief and fell back on the bed and triumphantly exclaimed "Yes!"

As You Like It

I am thrilled I had not overslept, and I did not have him waiting for me, wondering where I might be. I went in the bathroom, ran my bath water, and headed to the closet to decide what I would wear. I wanted something nice and sexy. This should probably be something, which will surely have him unable to keep his hands off of me. I wanted it to accentuate my nicely shaped legs and have him thinking about admiring them, constantly.

I smiled to myself as I thought about when we would finally be alone and how I wanted to make him feel. I snapped back into things and went in the tub. The warm, scented bubbles were soothing to my sensuous body. I relaxed and closed my eyes, trying to imagine him scooping me up in his arms and kissing me, passionately.

I put on my favorite lotion and perfume after my bath. I slid into the dress I had chosen to wear and combed my hair in a way that would have him ready to run his fingers through it. I grabbed my purse and headed out to the airport. I was nervous and excited at the same time.

I cannot believe we were actually getting ready to meet. I parked and quickly walked into the airport. I went over to the board and checked his flight status. I saw it was on time. I checked the arrival gate again to ensure all of the information he gave me was still the same.

I approached the gate where he was supposed to arrive, and I sat for a while, trying to not look as nervous as I felt. I stood and walked briefly to collect my thoughts.

"Attention in the concourse, Flight 513 from Chicago has arrived. Those passengers will be unloading here at gate 32C in approximately ten minutes. Again, Flight 513 from Chicago has arrived and will be unloading passengers in approximately 10 minutes. Thank you." My heart skipped a beat when I heard this. I was about to scream. I hurried over to a nearby restroom, checked my make-up, and touched up my hair.

When I came back out, I saw the people who were waiting for passengers had gathered around the gate. I walked over and tried to think of what I would say or what I would do. It seemed like I was there for about five minutes when our eyes met. I was about to flip out. My eyes had fallen on this tall, dark, handsome man in full military dress.

Be still my heart! Goodness gracious! He walked with such pride and authority; I am almost too scared to move towards him. I smiled a nice, little, seductive smile. He responded and quickened his pace.

I was unaware of anyone else at that time. I rushed into his arms and wrapped mine around him in a way, which would not allow them to be easily taken away. We looked into each other's eyes, and he said "Hi baby, I love you."

By now, tears were flowing freely from my eyes, and I am stumbling for words to say, but I managed a very teary, "I love you, more." We kissed and the world stopped revolving for a moment. His lips were very soft and inviting. He kissed me lightly at first. Then, he unleashed all of his passion upon me.

We were interrupted by an outburst of applause and cheering. We stopped and looked around to see everyone was paying more attention to us than we realized. We laughed and tried to shake off the embarrassment.

An older man approached us, extended his hand and said "thank you" to Ken. Ken shook his hand, but before he could ask the man why, he continued, "I'm thanking you for your service to this country. I'm a Vietnam Vet, and I wanted to give you something that we didn't all get when we got back home."

Accordingly, Ken stood at attention and saluted the older gentleman and said, "No, *thank you*, for *your* service to this country. It's an honor to be in your presence, sir." The gentleman was in absolute awe of Ken's display of respect. Tears brimmed his eyes as he said, "God bless you, son."

A girl who appeared to be in her late teens walked over and asked Ken and the gentleman if she could take a picture of them, together. The two men agreed, and the others in the area began to shout "thank you!" to Ken and the older gentleman as we walked away. That was an experience I do not think I will ever forget, and it was not by far one I WANT to forget. I walked out with this gorgeous man as he held me and acted like he did not want to let go, and quite frankly, neither did I.

My Baby

I did not really like the idea of sharing mommy and Daddy with anyone else, but I guess it would not be up to me in a few more days. My little brother will have been born, and I had to get used to sharing them and everything else, which was exclusively mine.

I was glad I was girl though because this would keep some things just for me. I got angry when I thought about how mommy would not be able to lie in bed next to me until I fell asleep, anymore. Daddy would not be calling me his "favorite" either. I guessed. Ewwww! Just the thought of getting less at Christmas and for my birthday had me ready to throw a major tantrum!

Why did snotty-nosed babies have to come along, anyway? How come the older sisters or brothers could not have say in whether or not siblings could be part of the family? I angrily threw my doll against the door and buried my head in my pillow to cry.

Grammy, the name I used for my father's mother, had told me my thoughts were selfish, but I could not help it. I had been the "baby" for eight years, and I did not want to lose all of the fun things or mommy and Daddy's attention. I knew she would ask me to do this and to do that and to do this again, but I did not want to do anything to make this baby feel welcome. I wanted him to go away and let me have my mom and Dad back and all to myself.

"Charity, what was that noise sweetie? Are you okay?" Mom must have heard the doll hit the door. I hurried to answer her, so she would not come into my room and see my crying.

"Uhhh...Uhhh...Yes, I'm okay, mommy. I accidentally fell when I was being silly in my room." I listened to see if she might come to me anyway, but she did not. She only called back to me.

"Okay! Please, be careful. You know I want you to be fit and ready to greet the baby when he comes in a few days." *Arrrgh!* She had to mention him, again. How come she could not just have him without involving me? I buried my head beneath my pillow and cried myself to sleep. It looked like I would be doing a lot of that from now on.

"Charity! Are you up yet, Pumpkin?" I heard Daddy walking towards my room. I had just finished brushing my teeth and putting on the clothes mom had laid out for me. I guess she will not be able to do that, anymore either.

"Yes, Daddy, I'm up and ready for us to go to the park." I rushed out into the hallway to meet him, but the look on his face informed me it would not be happening. He stooped down and scooped me up in his arms.

"Pumpkin, we're going to have to postpone the trip to the park. I'm going to have to go with mommy to the doctor's office. Once we get through there, we'll see what we still have time for. Grammy is going to come and be with you while we get this taken care of. Is that a deal?"

My eyes were burning with the tears, which were about to come gushing out of them. I am mad as a lizard, and I do not want this stinky baby taking anymore of mommy and Daddy's time.

"I don't like this baby! I don't like it that you and mommy are changing all of our plans because of him. Why did y'all have to have another one? Why?" I jumped down and ran into my room. I kicked my shoes off and tore at my clothes. He came in behind me. There was a pitiful look on his face, but I did not care. He came over and tried to put his hand on my shoulder, but I moved away. He looked down and walked out.

I crawled up into my bed and turned on the television. I heard them talking to Grammy as they left, and I am glad I had her to myself, at least for now. She peeked in at me. The smile on her face had always been enough to drown my boo-boos or other sad times. She came over and sat on the edge of my bed.

"Wanna tell Grammy all about it? I hear that you're not doing so well with accepting the new baby." I was sniffling and shivering because I had been crying so hard.

"Gram...Gram...Grammy, you don't understand. I've had mommy and Daddy all to myself, and now a baby wants to come along and spoil it. Why can't he go to another family?" Grammy said nothing. She sat there and let me go on and on and on.

Finally, she said, "Charity, you don't like the thought of being a big sister, but I can remember a time when an older sister was happy when you came along."

When she said this, I looked at her like she had been drinking some "joy juice" or smoking some of that stuff I have heard about at school. I began to ease over to her, and the tears started slowing, along with the "shakes" I seemed to be having as a result of the crying spell.

"Grammy? What are you talking about?" I asked and waited for her to finish looking for words (at least that's what mommy and Daddy call it).

A sad look came upon her face, and she pulled me into her lap. "Char, all this time you've been thinking that you're mommy and Daddy's first child and you're not, you're their second.

You had an older sister named Faith. She passed away when you were two-years-old, and you don't remember her. She loved you. She wanted to help mommy do everything when it came to you. She'd hold your bottle, wipe your bottom, and even laugh when you'd spit up on her."

My eyes got bigger, and I felt something funny in my stomach. I do not know what it was, but it had me feeling a little sick.

"Grammy, are you sure? Mommy and Daddy haven't mentioned her to me. How did she die? Why can't I remember her? How old was she when she died?" Grammy took a deep breath and said, "I'm very sure of it, Pumpkin. They haven’t mentioned her because they didn't want to force you to remember at this young age. They wanted to see if you'd remember her on your own, and then they were going to fill you in on all that happened. One day while she was out riding her bike, she fell and hit her head and she never woke up, again. She was about to be ten in a couple more months."

"Grammy, you...you...said that she liked doing things for me, and that she liked helping mommy take care of me?" Grammy nodded her head.

"Yes, she adored you. She was so glad that she had someone to share things with and to laugh and talk to. You were a baby and didn't understand, but you were another 'little person,' and that way, she wasn't with adults all of the time. She couldn't wait for you to get big enough to take you to the park or to play dolls with you."

I dropped my head and began to cry some more. She wrapped her arms around me tighter.

"Char, do you think that you could ever get used to having a new baby around? What would it take for you to try?" I looked up at her, my vision blurred because the tears began to pour from my eyes, continuously.

"Grammy, I told Daddy that I didn't want the baby. I told him that I wished he could have gone to a different family. I think I hurt his feelings." Grammy was crying now, but she was doing her best to hide her pain from me.

"Char, mommy and Daddy are at the hospital because she's having problems and the baby...ummm the baby...the baby might not make it. Do you understand that?" I jumped up and ran to the corner of the room. I put my fingers in my ears. I did not want to hear Grammy say this.

"Noooo Grammy! Nooo Grammy! It's my fault! I did this! I don't want to be bad, and I don't want mommy and Daddy to be sad. Grammy, will God hear me if I say something good about the baby? Please Grammy!"

Grammy hurried over to me, and we cried for a few minutes. I asked her about how God could hear us when we said things. I told her HE must have heard everything I said about the baby, and HE was giving me what I wanted. I was sorry, now. I felt really bad in my stomach. It felt like I might throw up. Grammy wiped my tears away and said, "Char, God always hears us, and HE always acts according to HIS will. If it is meant for the baby to leave...HE will. If God wants to keep him here a little longer, HE'LL do that too, but we won't know until we hear from your mom and Dad."

"Mom and Dad?"

I ran to my closet and started putting on clothes. I went in, washed my face, and stepped out to put on my shoes. Grammy stood and asked, "What are you doing? Where are you going Char?" I turned to her and said, "Come on Grammy, we have to go to the doctor's office. I have to let mommy and Daddy know that I'm sorry. I have to do right. Isn't that what you've always taught me, Grammy?" She smiled and said, "Yes baby, it is. Okay, we can do that. Hold on. Let me get my purse and shoes." We ran to the car and started out to join mommy and Daddy. The ride seemed long, but this was okay with me because I used the time to talk to God, and I asked Him to let mommy and Daddy keep the baby.

The parking garage was big and scary looking, but I was not going to let anything keep me from reaching them. I grabbed her hand, and we walked really quickly into the building. She told a lady, who was sitting behind a desk, whom we were looking for, and we went to the elevators to find them. I hated the way it stopped all of a sudden and made my stomach jump. It opened on the fourth floor and we walked out, looking for the number the lady at the desk gave us. I was almost dragging Grammy, but she did not seem to mind.

I saw other people crying, holding sick children, and walking back and forth. I guess they were waiting to see the doctor. It looked so clean. The floor was shiny, and it smelled kind of funny. I'm glad I wore jeans and long sleeves. It was cold in here, too.

We turned about two corners (I thought), and then, we were looking down a long hallway. We walked up to the desk, and I heard Daddy's voice.

"Grammy, we are in here." We turned and saw him standing outside a room. I ran to him, and he lifted me up with the biggest hug.

"Daddy, I'm so sorry. I didn't mean all of those things that I said, and I do want you and mommy to be able to keep the baby. Are you mad at me?" He buried me in his chest and said, "No Pumpkin, I'm not mad at you, and I understand about having someone new to come along, but don't you know that there's enough of mommy and me to go around? The baby's here. Do you want to see him?" I pulled myself back from his arms, looked at him in surprise, and said, "He's here? I thought it would be a few more days?" He looked over at Grammy, who was crying harder than I was, and she looked like she was saying a quiet prayer to God.

"Yes, he's here, and as soon as they tell me I can, I'm going to go in and see him. Do you want to go in with me?" I looked over at Grammy. She was smiling deeply and shaking her head like she does when I am being a big girl and making her proud.

"Yes Daddy! I want to go, but first, can I see mommy?" He squatted down and explained to me they had to do a special procedure on mommy, and it made her really tired. He said she would be oblivious to my presence from sleeping, anyway.

A nice lady came over afterwards and escorted us to the big, baby room. Numerous new babies were there. Daddy tapped on the window, and a nurse came over to look at the identification band on his arm. She went to the corner and pushed a really curly haired, baby boy over to the window. Daddy lifted me up, so I could see him, better. He was *so* cute! He was moving his little hands and blinking his little eyes. *Geesh!* He was smaller than some of my baby dolls at home.

"Hey you...Hey you...I'm your big sister. I hope you'll like me just like our big sister liked me."

Daddy put me down, went over, and hugged Grammy when I said this. They cried for a little bit. I guess he knew that she had to have told me about the sister who left us. I ran over and pulled at his arm.

"Hey Daddy, what's his name? You never told me his name." He put his hand to his chin and said, "Well, mommy and I were hoping that you would help us out with that. Since he's your baby, we thought that you might have a good one for him."

"*What!* I'm going to name him? He's my baby?" He nodded his head, and I ran back to the window to see what great name was in his eyes. I could not name him just any old thing. I wanted Grammy and everyone to be proud of him, and not just because he was a snotty-nosed, little boy either, but because he was *my* baby.

Baby Girl's Sad Dose of Reality

I decided to make a quick run to the grocery store after picking my sixteen-year-old up from STEP practice. After shopping and heading home, we noticed a man standing on the corner with a sign that read "HUNGRY AND HOMELESS. ANYTHING YOU CAN SPARE WILL HELP. GOD BLESS YOU." I looked over at the warm, juicy, oven-roasted chicken we had just bought and had our hearts set on eating.

"Hand me that chicken, baby girl." She looked a little puzzled at first; it was almost as if she were daring me to pop the top and start devouring it.

I looked at her out the corner of my eye and said, "Dang! I want to give this to that man, but our light just changed." She said nothing but her eyes probed him. She looked at him from head to toe. He was grubby in appearance. His hair was held flat by a baseball cap, and his eyes were dark, sad, and pleading.

"*Oh Mommy!* How's he going to get it?" I glanced in my rearview mirror and noticed there were not too many cars behind me but enough to raise hell if they were in a hurry.

"They'll just have to wait, I guess." I accelerated slowly and held my left arm out of the window with the chicken in my hand.

"Sir?" I called out. He turned, saw what I was holding, and hurried to the car. He smiled and tilted his head in an appreciative manner.

"Thank you ma'am and *God bless you!"* I smiled and turned the corner. I glanced back and saw him immediately drop to the ground to tear into the package before losing him, totally.

I was startled when stifled noises came from the direction of my daughter. I looked over at her and saw tears streaming down her face.

"You *okay*?" I asked. She lost control and spoke between labored breaths. She said, "Mommy that is so sad. How can that be?" I did not know what to tell her because I don't know that *I knew* what to tell her.

"Baby girl, life is strange. It's full of riddles and things that boggle the mind. I know that's hard for you to understand, but you go ahead and cry for him and all of the others like him because you hurting and showing compassion for him might be what helps the Creator show mercy on you and yours if there's ever a time that it's needed."

I *could not* console her at this point because she needed to deal with this as best as she could in her own way. I took a long trip back to when I was younger, and my mother shielded me from seeing people on the streets or heart-wrenching things because my reaction was the same as my daughter's.

I remembered my mother wondering aloud why God had made me so sensitive and destined for a tormented life. I *did not* think she ever found the answer, and Heaven *knew* I still *cried* for those less fortunate than myself. Therefore, I have not found it, either.

I decided I was unable to return home unless I brought him more to eat, so we arrived at a different store and pondered items that would "keep" and carry him for a day or two.

"Baby girl, go and get some cookies. How about a jug of juice? Yes, he'll need little wipes and bread. Do I need to get chips and another eight pieces of chicken?"

We hurried around the store as it was getting ready to rain, and I did not know how long he might be under the freeway. We paid for his things. I got a bag out of the trunk and neatly placed all of the food items in it.

I was careful to purchase lightweight things, so my "care package" would not be an added burden.

"You keep looking to see if you see him while I try to decide where to turn and hand it to him." She continued to wipe the tears from her eyes and looked to and fro for him.

He was not there. I turned and doubled the corner without any sign of him.

"*Aw mommy!* He's gone." She began to cry, again. My heart ached for her, but there was nothing that I could do.

"All is not lost baby. When we get home, don't take anything out of the car but the chicken. Everything else we'll keep. We can come back tomorrow and give it to him."

She perked up and seemingly handled it better, knowing I would not forget about him, so quickly. After a couple minutes of silence I said, "Girl, we weren't gone that long and how far could he have gotten? Wouldn't it be awesome if we just fed the 'Master'?"

She sat up on her legs and said, "*Mommy!* I was just sitting here thinking that! You never know when you're hosting '*angels*'." We had a comforting little laugh, which helped soothe both of our hearts, but I know one way to find out. *I will* go back tomorrow at the same time, the same corner, and with the same heart...He will be there. We went back on the way home from one of her Step Shows (they took second place with a trophy and $250 prize), but he was not there. We ran into our same, little friend whom we had fed last week. She spotted him first, and her eyes lit up.

"Mommy! Look! It's *him*! Dang! We don't have anything in the car to give him, either."

"Not to worry baby girl. I'll holla at him as we pass by." She was still sitting on the edge of her seat and watching the light turn green on us, *again*.

What is it with these green lights catching me when I *need* to stop? As we got closer to him, I yelled out the window, "Stay right here. We'll be back with something for you in about ten minutes. Will you be here?"

He looked at us as we're passing and nodded his head, questionably. We flew to the store.

"*Okay* baby girl! You know the routine. Run and get, and I'll run and get. Meet me at the register."

We ran and got, ran and got, and met at the

register. We made a mad dash out and went back to where he was. Guess what? He was *still* there.

We handed him the basket of food, and I told him I hoped he would not have trouble carrying it since I had gotten him a couple days' worth of "rations." You know things which will keep for two or three days at least: chicken, bread, crackers, chips, juice, beef jerky, apples, bananas, candy.

He bent down and looked into the car as if he expected it to be a belated April Fool's joke or something. He took it, bid us a good night with "GOD BLESS YOU," and we were on our way. No sounds from the daughter this time. I looked over, and she was cheesing from ear to ear.

"Baby girl, you liked that, didn't you?"

"Yes, Mommy, he was so thankful. I'm glad we saw him, again. Aren't you?"

"Yes, I was, and let's make a deal, right now. Let's make it a promise that every week when we are out and about, we'll feed one of the people who we might see standing on the corner asking for help. We can't do all of them, but looking out for one can have the same impact as looking out for many."

She perked up and smiled. Her hazel eyes glistened in the nightlight, which shone through the car window.

"Cool, I like that."

Shoot, we eat out at least twice a week, or rent a movie, or do some other recreation, so sacrificing one or the other to be sure someone has eaten is a small price to pay.

As You Like It

I forgot to mention I prayed over the basket of food on the way to the car before giving it to him. I asked for it to nourish his body. Plus, I prayed he found a way to have brighter days. Furthermore, I also asked God for my act of kindness toward him to cause someone to extend acts of kindness to my friend's son: he has been a missing runaway for nine days, now.

Friends Like This - Part I

Several weeks have passed since I dropped Melissa off in a faraway land, but she continued to communicate with me through a mutual friend. The friend hoped I get to the point where I could talk to her soon. She felt the need to "explain" a few things to me.

What exactly is she not understanding? I am doing very well, and there's nothing to talk about. What in the entire hell made her think "friends" could mistreat one another and resume life as though nothing ever happened?

Hell, it was not like she borrowed money and failed to repay it. It was not like she had forgotten to invite me to her child's birthday party. *She* was directly involved in covering up, aiding and abetting, and totally disrespecting baby girl and I by co-signing on the affair between her delusional sister and *my* husband.

The irony was I made sure she and their son had food to eat when the sorry-tailed man, whom she was married to, was beating her down and running off for weeks at a time. Whose blood boiled when I recalled the time I got ready to straight up be up in his dental work because of the way he had treated her in addition to his exposed cowardice upon leaving her while she was in the hospital? Yet, she could deal me a hand like this.

He had not done jack to me, but I ran up on him and dared him to hit me because *she* was my "friend," and I could imagine how it must have felt to come home from the hospital and see the man who has sworn to stick by you has hauled tail. I went ahead and rose up out of their house because she was still returning to him after all was said and done. I was out of line, but he knew I was not the one to be messed with.

Darn it! Jamal is here! I was enjoying this moment of reflection, but I better get up and get Sasha ready. It was his weekend with her, and I totally ignored the time. I got up and glanced in the mirror before I opened the door. A sister was not getting caught slipping in her appearance. I suspect he would have really enjoyed believing I was slowly but surely going downhill. Not today. I took a deep breath and opened the door.

"Hey Jamal. Come on in. I haven't finished getting her ready yet because she's still asleep. Give me a minute." I walked into her bedroom. I was slowly dressing her, and I was startled upon feeling him brush up against me.

"Whoa dude! You need to move around. You almost caught one." He smacked his lips and said, "You make it seem like it's been a lifetime since we were together." He reached up and brushed a curl from my face.

"Who are you getting all cute for?"

"I know it's been a minute since you cared to realize it, but I've *always* been cute and since you are where you are and I am where I am, it really isn't any of your business *who* I spend time with as long as I keep it away from the baby." He stepped back with his hands in the air.

"Hey, hey, hey...I'm not trying to get off into that with you. I was just trying to soften the mood and get you to loosen up a bit. I'm sorry for asking."

"You just ought to be. "Loosen up" *hell.* You were prying and trying to see whether or not I'm finding someone else to keep me occupied while you're out there, but you'll never know. Grab her bag right there, and I'll help you out to your car with her."

I picked her up and looked into her innocent, little face as she began to snap out of her peaceful sleep. She smiled when she felt me kissing her nose and whisper "I love you" in her ear. Her eyes were wide when I spoke to her.

"Daddy's here. You'll be with him for a little bit, *okay*?" She *strained* her neck in an effort to look for him. He approached me from behind and placed her hand in his.

"Hey baby. How's Daddy's girl doing? Did mommy wake you up? Did Mommy wake you up?" She smiled and reached for him. For some reason, this particular time he came for her bothered me. I gave her to him and quickly walked out of the room. I went into the kitchen and packed a few things for her to eat and turned to see them both standing there looking at me.

"Hey girl, you *okay*?" I smacked my lips and shot back "Why wouldn't I be?" He followed with "I was just checking. You left out of the room kinda fast, and I wanted to be sure that you were all right." I wanted to be mindful of Sasha, but he was working my darn nerves.

"Look Jamal, you can cut it with the fake concern and things for me. I'm going to be fine. What doesn't kill me will make me stronger, and this *too* shall pass. Do *you* and let me do *me*, but until we have legally gone our separate ways, don't allow yourself to be troubled by me. Common sense tells me that if it meant *tha*t much to you, *we* wouldn't be in the predicament that we are in. Understood?"

He lifted her bag up and said, "Whatever. Yo, we're outta here. I'll have her back by about 3:00 on Sunday." I walked them to the door and gave her a big kiss before they left.

"Mommy loves you, and I'll see you, later." I went to the window and watched them as they drove off and then I cried. I did not know exactly why I did, but I just lost it. In the midst of that storm the phone rings...it's him.

"Hey, I forgot to tell you that Melissa begged me to ask you to give her a call. I know that it's out of order and how you might feel about it, but I really do believe that she misses you, Angel." I can say nothing. I am not even in the mood to do this with him.

"Jamal, I'm not calling her today, tomorrow, or *ever*. What's done is done, and I can't see going back. You were with me long enough to know that I only allow a person one time to mess over me the way that she did and then all bets are off. If you believe you can bring yourself to do it, you can tell her that there will be no need to send anymore messages through you, Claire, Moses, Mary Magdalene, or Simon Peter. It's over! I'm fine and I don't care to be her friend anymore, even though I won't burn in hell for hating her either."

He was silent for a moment and then said, "Angel, I know this doesn't mean much, but I am sorry. I don't know what I could say to make you believe that, and I don't know what I was thinking when I did what I did. I don't know that I could ever make it right, but I did want you to know that. Being there with y'all today kinda spooked me. She has always been ready for me when I've come to get her and seeing you dress and interact with her as you did...it just made me think."

"I appreciate the apology, and if you meant it, I hope that it'll be an experience that you never want to repeat. There won't be any winners in this whether we come back together and try it again or end it, amicably. The first cut is the deepest, and trust is one of the hardest things in the world to regain, once it's lost. I guess all we can hope for is that regardless of what happens with us, Sasha will remain an unconditional priority for *both* of us."

"Angel, I'm scared. I'm frustrated, and I'm unsure of what the future holds, but I can't say one way or another: what's best for us. What are we supposed to do?"

I shook my head and felt sorry for him at the same time. Jamal might be confused, frustrated, and a lot of things, but he had always been a hard worker and provided a very good life for us. I had been showered with the best of a lot of things, but that was not enough to neutralize the hurt and pain that his breaking our vows had inflicted upon me.

"Jamal, all we can do is what we're doing, which is take it one day at a time and make sure that we have thought this thing out, thoroughly. However, I do want you to know that I will not remain in limbo, indefinitely."

"Does that mean that you have a time frame in mind now, or that you already know what you want to do?" he asked.

"No Jamal. It means that we'll know when we know."

Friends Like This - Part II

The phone rang three times, and I was tempted to hang up. It was past midnight, and I did not want to disturb Jamal if he was already in bed. He would have to be ready for work in less than six hours. I did not want to be the reason he lost any sleep, nor did I want to deal with Marge. I removed the phone from my ear and proceeded to hang up when I heard her drowsy voice, "Hello?" It took me a split second to decide I would not hang up on her. After all, I did call her home, and it really was not warranted. I gathered the nerve to ask for him, anyway. "Hi, this is Angel and I know that it's late, but I have an emergency. Is Jamal there?"

There was dead silence for a few minutes, and I wondered if she had fallen asleep or had simply laid the phone down with no intentions of letting him know that it was me. She sighed deeply and then said, "Where else would he be? He's asleep."

I bit my lip and started counting to about ten thousand. This heifer was in a messed-up mood, and I was not in a frame of mind to entertain her. I was not sure how to take her last comment, but I was on a mission and replied, "I meant nothing by that. It's natural when calling someone's home to ask if they are there."

She hastily replied, "Can I give him a message for you, or is that something you would want to do yourself?" I knew it was time for me to get off and I countered with "Yes, you can give him a message for me. Can you tell him that I'm in the emergency room at Peter's Memorial Hospital? Sasha has chickenpox and is running a high fever. I'll need him to get back with me as soon as he can. I have my cell phone with me. I'm sorry to have disturbed you."

"Oh! In that case hold on. I'll be sure that he gets up." I was so damned heated by this time that I did not wait. I hung the phone up and went back into her room: they were still trying to lower Sasha's temperature. When I entered the room, the nurse was feeding her ice chips. I walked over, took Sasha's little hand in mine, kissed it, and asked the nurse a question.

"Has it gone down any?" She smiled at me and said, "Yes, but not enough for you to go home just yet. If we can get it down within the hour, Dr. Ratcliff will let you take her home. I have packaged up samples of medicine that you can bathe her in. It'll make things considerably more comfortable for her while the pox run their course."

Sasha was just lying there with no set expression or exact demeanor. She whimpered and twisted her little body in an effort to relieve herself of the itching and irritation. All I could do was stand helplessly and hoped it was short lived. The nurse leaned over and patted my hand.

"Hang in there, kiddo. She's going to be okay. I'm a mother and know how you feel. I suffered right along with my kids when they were going through their childhood illnesses and things. That's part of the reason that I went back to nursing school. I wanted to be able to soothe, make better, and otherwise alleviate their pains." I felt comfort from her sharing that with me. I smiled at her as the tears slowly began to trickle down my face.

"Why don't you go and stretch out over there, and she will be okay. The medicine the doctor had me give her will have her in 'sleepy land' in a few minutes. Rest yourself." God was smiling on me. He knew I needed this. After she said this, I went over to the cot near the window, climbed upon it, and silently prayed for the fever to break. I was near dozing when the nurse came over and lightly shook me.

"Mrs. Heath, there's a gentleman here who says he's your husband, should I show him back?" I didn't make one move. I was so beat that I thought I was imagining it. A firmer shake by her was indication that this was real and that Jamal was outside. I sat up and straightened my clothes.

"Yes, please show him back. Thank you." Once she left the room, I went over to the sink, straightened my hair, and drunk some water to rid myself of the dry mouth, which plagued me.

I was gently rubbing my hand through Sasha's hair when he entered. He eased closer to prevent disturbing her. He placed his hand on my arm and whispered, "What's going on?" I released her hand from mine, and we stepped over to another part of the room to talk.

"She has chickenpox and tonight her fever was at a hundred and two, so I brought her in. They're still trying to get it down now, or I won't be able to take her home." He looked over at her and a pitiful look came over his face. He turned back to me.

"Why didn't you call me before y'all left the house? I would have come and picked y'all up. It's late and I'm not too particular about y'all being out here like this." I was appreciative of this and told him.

"Jamal, it means a lot to me that you'd think enough of me to do that, but I didn't want to disturb you and Marge. In fact, the only reason that I called was because they're going to call in a couple of prescriptions for her, and I left my checkbook at home. I'll need you to get them for me, and I can pay you back on Friday." He smacked his lips and testily replied, "The only reason? You weren't going to tell me that she was sick?" I put my finger to my mouth and pointed him out the door. I stayed where I could see her if she stirred and said to him,

"Yes I was going to tell you. I meant the only reason that I called tonight because, as it turns out, it doesn't look like Marge was happy that I called and I wanted to avoid that, but with her needing prescriptions I took the chance, anyway. You know I haven't been in your business since we went our separate ways, but could you find it in your heart to tell ya' girl not to piss around with me where Sasha is concerned?" He placed his hands on his hips and gave me a blank stare while saying, "What are you talking about?"

I was not ready to do this with him, and I did not know whether or not he really knew how the call went, but I decided to explain in the process of giving him the benefit of the doubt.

"When I called, she pretended that she tried to get you up and couldn't. Not until I told her that Sasha was sick, and I was in the ER did she make an honest attempt to get you up. That was why I didn't wait for you to get back on the phone. I was heated and didn't want to bring discord between you—." He walked closer to me and narrowed his eyes.

"*If* my child is sick, I don't give a damn *who* I am with...You call me! I'll set her straight on that, but you and I made a promise that OUR daughter would always come first, and I meant every word of that. Do you understand that, Angel?"

I had fronted long enough and was too tired to fight it. I burst out crying, and he appeared shock and bewildered as if wondering what to do. I leaned against the wall and cried. He came over and hugged me. I do not mean a scared, apprehensive hug either. It was a firm, supportive, and caring hug. My hands were on my face before he removed them. He brushed my hair back from my face and asked me to look at him.

"Angel, I know you're tired, and I know how you've always worried about her when she was sick, but *no one* will ever get in the way of my being there for *both* of you when you're faced with something like this. Marge was out of line, and I'm going to tell her, but I don't want you to let that stop you from contacting me when you need to. *Okay*?"

I smiled at him and returned his hug. The nurse interrupted us to let us know Sasha's fever had broken, and we could take her home. I entered the room and dressed her. The medicine started working, and she would be out for a good little while.

I was so pleased. She had not slept in what seemed like twenty-four hours, and I was beside myself. The nurse came over and handed me two bottles of medication. I looked inquisitively at her and she whispered, "These are samples of the prescriptions that Dr. Ratcliff is going to give you. You are worn out. These will come in handy over the next couple of days. Get home and get in the bed. Get the others filled as soon as possible. At the window on your way out, they'll have your discharge instructions and the prescriptions. Y'all take care and have a good night." I thanked her, and she left us in the room to finish gathering Sasha.

"Angel, I'm going to follow y'all home. It's too late for y'all to be traveling and you're pooped. I wanna be sure that y'all get there, *okay*." That was fine with me. I did not feel like driving, but I could drive safely knowing he would be there to prevent my fatigue from killing me.

We made it home after what seemed eternity. He told me to enter the house while he gathered her. I entered, started her little music, and prepared her for bed. I sat at the end while he stretched her upon it. I turned to pull her clothes off of her and he said, "I got this, gone ahead to bed. I'll let myself out." I obeyed every word like a child. I went into the room and pulled my blouse off. I sat on the bed to take my shoes off, and that was all she wrote.

I was awakened by Jamal’s hands upon me. He was taking my shoes off and talking to me as he did so.

"Angel...Angel, wake up and get outta ya' clothes." I stood up and unbuttoned by jeans and let them fall to my feet after they were free. He pulled them off of me once they hit my ankles. I slid back onto the bed and recaptured my stolen moments of sleep when I felt him crawl up next to me. He played in my hair at first and slid his hand to my shoulder. He traced my bra with one of his fingers and then undid it.

It was such a relief to be free from it. It felt as though I had been in it for three days. He massaged the area where it left lines and then licked them. I was feeling him and what he was doing to me, but I knew I should not let this happen. So, I was going to do all that I could to fight it.

I guess in my mind, the fact that I was still his wife allowed me to welcome him in as payback for a scandalous trick that made me pull her "hoe-card," but the love I had for myself made it easier for me to thank him kindly and send him on his way.

Friends Like This - III

My nice, warm, bubble bath was interrupted by the sound of the phone ringing. I glanced over at the countertop to see I had forgotten to bring it with me. I sat for a moment, trying to decide whether or not I would answer it. The candles' flicker and soft glow had relaxed me so much; all I wanted to do was lose myself in the therapeutic feeling of this bath. It had been a while since I pampered myself this way. I finally decided to let the answering machine catch it. I was not ready to give up this free time.

After all, the past two weeks have been hell on me, and I wanted to get in as much "me" time as possible. Sasha had finally gotten over chickenpox, and she would be with Jamal for at least another three or four hours. So, it is all about me, right now.

The bath pillow he bought me for Mother's Day last year was one of the best investments he had ever made. Stretching out and dozing (while getting an invigorating bath) had been made so much nicer with it. It had different settings that allowed a gentle massage to work while my body absorbed the milk-and-honey bath scent I had sprinkled into the water. It was a wonder I had not slid off in here and drowned with the way I lose myself.

The phone rang, again. This time I decided to answer it, so I rose from the bath and headed to it while I wrapped a towel around myself, simultaneously.

"Hello? It is Janice," she starts in, immediately.

"Hey Angel! I got your message the other night, and I wanted to tell you that you are a certifiable nut, but I'm damn sure with you on this one." That trick had some nerve to try and keep you from talking to Jamal until she learned that Sha-Sha was sick. She's an insecure little wench!"

I laughed when she said that. Janice was as low-key and as docile as they came, but she can come on up out of the bag on ya when the wrong nerve was struck.

"I shoulda let you kick her butt when we saw her and Jamal at that darn hotel that night." I dropped on the bed when she said this and enjoyed a good laugh, loudly. She became silent and then asked a question.

"Angel, what in the hell is so funny?" I placed my hand upon my chest, tried to catch my breath, and said, "Girl, I ain't heard you talk like this in a long time. She really ran you hot, huh?"

She sucked her teeth and said, "Girl, you don't play about people's darn children. That's a 'no-no' and will get ya' butt tow up!" She continued to talk. I looked around and saw the message light on the answering machine was blinking. This had to be the call, which came in while I was in the tub. I pushed the button to hear it and reclined on the bed while Janice talked to me about work, her new haircut, and their trip to Tahiti.

I sprung up with quickness when I heard the voice.

"Uh, Angel, this is Marge and I wanted to say that I was *not* trying to keep you from speaking to Jamal the other night when you called to tell him about Sasha. He was tired, and I wanted him to sleep. I don't know what *you* told him happened, but I don't appreciate the way that he came off on me, and I figured you had to have added something to what I said..."

"*Angel!*" It scared the heck out of me when Janice yelled my name like that. I was so far gone in that message I had forgotten I was even talking to her.

"Girl, hold on a minute! You have to hear this. Marge called while I was in the tub and left me a throwed-off message. Jamal musta got in that bootay a little about not waking him up, immediately. Hold on…I'll play it for you."

"*Oh hell!* You mean to tell me that she had the nerve to call and try and get with you because he got on her?" She cackled like a wild woman.

"Man oh man! That heffa is runnin' scared. You got her, Angel! You got her! If he got on her, that means she knows that he must hold what you say in high regards," I interrupted her.

"Shhhh...Listen." I let the message play all the way to the end and saved it, just in case.

"Is that pathetic, or is that pathetic?" she asked.

"That's beyond pathetic, and it's all good because 'turnabout is fair play,'" I said, as I lay there waiting for her to ask me what that meant.

"*Okay*, you lost me there Angel, what does that

have to do with turnabout and fair play?" I let a very conniving and manipulative little giggle escape me.

"Angel! You didn't!" She screamed this at me and I dropped the phone on the bed. I laughed and rolled on it as her light and airy chuckle confirmed she now knew what I was talking about.

"You are too much! Girl! Did you work him good?" She asked with no embarrassment, whatsoever.

"I did nothing to him. He wanted me to, but I couldn't and that was how I got him. He is my husband, and I would be within my rights as his wife. But I wasn't going to give in to lust. As a matter of fact, hold on while I call her ignorant behind back. You stay quiet and don't say nothing,' *okay*?" I clicked over and dialed Jamal's house. I heard Janice snickering on her end. Marge answered.

"Marge, it's me Angel, and I was calling to clarify things with you. First of all, I didn't tell Jamal anything that *didn't* happen, so whatever was said between you two is not the result of my misrepresenting the truth. Secondly, there really was no need for you to call and say anything to me about it because that's y'all's thing and doesn't concern me. All I ask is that you be considerate enough to pass him the phone when I call for him. We have a child together, *I am* his wife, and until she becomes of age or we divorce, the contact will be there.

You can try and get used to it or suffer in silence, but never make the mistake of not letting me talk to him, again. Is *that* understood?"

She began to breathe heavily and started her tirade, "You're a lying ass bitch! You had to have told him something different for him to come in here like he did. You're one awful, got damned, sorry woman to have to use your daughter to get him to be around you, again! Is that what real women do?" I *was not* going to go there with her. My fight was won when I got her upset and going off like she was, but I was going to "checkmate" her really quickly, anyway.

"Ummm...I'm surprised that you used *real* and *woman* in the same sentence because if you were remotely aware of the meaning, you wouldn't have to tip with another woman's husband. If I'm his *real* wife, what does that make you? Good day." I hung up while she continued to talk.

When I clicked back over to talk with Janice, she was laughing so hard; she was wheezing.

"Angel, that girl is gonna have somebody take you out! Girl! You capped on her something fierce! I really think his getting on her has made her see something that she might not have had to worry about before, Angel. You think?"

I sat there for a moment with furrowed eyebrows and lost thought. I wished I could have been a fly on the wall. She made it seem like he issued out quite the punishment.

"I don't know, but she's crazy as hell. I wouldn't be calling a man's wife and telling her that she was the cause of him raining hell on me. She's desperate. That's all fine and well, but there won't be any talking next time, if she refuses to let me speak to him. Believe that."

"I hear ya', girl, but I better get off of here and get Jimmy and the boys something to eat. I was just calling to tell you that I got the message and could see why you were pissed. You got her good. I wouldn't even sweat it anymore after tonight." I laughed a confident laugh.

"Not me, but I'll talk to you later, Janice. Tell Jimmy and the boys that I said 'Hello.' " We ended the call, and I pulled the edge of the sheet over me. I did not bother getting up to put on clothes or anything. I just wanted to take a quick nap. For some reason, they always seemed to be what I needed to bring me back to myself and with as little work as possible to keep me there.

Made To Love Him

"You don't do me right." Greg and I were spooning when he whispered this into my ear. I thought he was kidding, but I began to feel that he meant it as I recalled how "bland" our time together seemed, lately. Still, I said nothing. I waited to give him the opportunity to bring it to the table if it was something that he really needed to talk about.

"See what I mean? I just brought a legitimate concern to you, and you continue to lie there as if I've said nothing." He released his hold on me and turned to face the wall. I was more irritated he broke our connection than I was with his obvious discontent. I looked forward to our time of holding one another. He would scoop me up and adjust his body to mine. I would be nestled perfectly between his chest and legs. I turned and faced him, placing a hand on his shoulder.

"Greg baby, I'm sorry. I didn't know that you were serious. Why do you say that I treat you badly?" He took a deep breath and began.

"Dalondra, I've given you my all. I've risked all to be with you, yet you still keep me at arm's length. You will not allow me totally into your space, and I feel that there's only so far you're going to allow me in and then 'poof'...just like that we're a done deal and it's over." He rolled over onto his back and stared at the ceiling.

I placed my hand on his chest and allowed my fingers to tiptoe through the slightly hairy, beautifully sculpted work of art, which caught my eye years ago, when we met at the gym.

"Baby, I'm...I'm sorry. I don't know what to tell you. I thought I had welcomed you totally into my space, but if you're feeling this way...I don't guess that I have. Is there anything in particular that has you feeling this way?"

He turned to face me now, and the look on his face had me feeling so ashamed. Greg had been very good to me. He had never given me reason to doubt his love for me nor given me a desire be anywhere else, but the fear of being hurt again must had been lurking in my mind more than I knew or was willing to admit. He had never forgotten a birthday, anniversary, Valentine's Day, Christmas, or the general causes when he showered me with acts of love and thoughtfulness. Every little detail of his life was mine for the asking. He kept nothing from me and asked very little of me.

"When we're talking, and I'm expressing very critical and valid points, you blow them off and trivialize them. You don't make me feel that you'd ever miss me if I were gone. I know that my heart skips a beat whenever I lay eyes on you or have the occasion to talk with you, but whenever I'm here, you just seem so distant, so unmoved by what we have. That hurts like hell. I love you more than anything I can think of, right now, and to know that it might never be returned is more than I can take." We lay there looking into one another's eyes, and I place my hand over his heart. It was racing and slowing down at the same time. This could very well be a figment of my imagination, but I was not going to let fear keep me from loving him totally, and I needed him to know that.

"Greg, I don't know what to say. I really have been trying to love you as you have me, but I had to have been fooling myself at your expense. Can you forgive me for that?" I placed my finger to his lips to quiet him as I continued to speak.

"We've been doing this for three years now, and I do love each and every little thing about you. My error has been in believing that it, rather than past pains, have been evident. I've been scared. I've been confused. I've been cautious, not wanting to hurt again. Not wanting to be totally alone again."

I started crying at this point. The thought of not having him in my life was swirling around in my head. Erasing three years of total bliss had me troubled. He pulled me closer to him and whispered, "Just love me. No past, no 'what if this' or 'what if that.' Just love me as best as you can, however you can, and while you can. That's all that I ask. Baby, I never wanted to be in love, again either. I never thought I would find anyone who'd make me want to be, but when we met and my heart wouldn't let me deny it any longer, I was willing to gamble."

He pulled me up and tucked me neatly away between his chest and legs. Spooning as we always had.

"Londra?"

I was dozing at this point, but I was going to let him know that this was a new time and place for us and our love.

"Yes baby?"

"Always?" he asked. I took his hand from my waist and placed it over my heart.

"Yes baby...Always."

None So Blind

The loud ringing of the phone startled me to the point of almost causing me to jump out of bed. I knew mother would answer it, but it is not the greatest sound in the world to wake up to when you are having a perfect sleep. I continued to lay there with the hope of resuming my sleep, but my racing heart let me know it would be a little longer before that happened.

My radio was still turned low, and the usual noises of the morning had not begun yet. Therefore, I heard her soft, reassuring voice, clearly. I did not know who it was, but I could tell that it was an important call because she repeatedly stated, "I see…That's remarkable…I don't know what to say…"

I realized I would not be resuming my sleep, so I lay there and listened to the wonderful ever present sounds of nature outside of my window. The birds chirped and sang a chorus, which drew you into their lively and busy, little lives. The flowers were in full bloom during this time of year, and they released their potent and seductive scents. The screeching halts and honking horns of some passing cars reminded me of a symphony: each musical instrument had its own purpose and completed whatever piece was gracing the listener's ear.

I decided to get a little closer to the action on this particular morning. I pushed the covers back and swung my legs to the bedside. I eased down until my feet felt the soft, fluffy material of my slippers. I could not help but smile when I made contact. Mom washed the indoor shoes once a week and promised to share her secret about how their 'fluff' seemed to last so long.

I slowly stood and searched my immediate left for something else that was an absolute. I was quite beat last night when I fell asleep, but I ensured it was within reach. I touched the wall and ran my hands down it until I felt the handle. I positioned myself firmly and made my way to the window.

All of my steps were numbered with rather precise and calculated movements. I did not need my cane as much in my bedroom, but having everything in functioning order upon awakening was not always the case.

I brushed the chair that Dad had placed near the window and maneuvered myself into it while placing the cane against the wall. I stuck one foot out and felt for the footrest, which was always there. I pulled it closer and placed both feet on it upon finding it.

I sunk into the chair and observed everything, which enticed me from lying in bed, earlier. I heard the neighbors screen door slam as their children ran to the car being driven to school. Their giggles and excitement suggested they loved this ritual as well as attending school.

My serenity was disturbed by my mother's voice.

“Yes, I’ll get back to you as soon as I’ve had the opportunity to speak with my husband and Janelle about this. Thank you so much, Dr. Bosh.” She hung up and made her way to my room. She knocked lightly and spoke.

“Good morning Janelle, are you awake?”

I turned toward the sound of her voice and said, “Good morning mother. Yes, the phone’s ringing awoke me.” I could feel her coming closer to me, and I was curious about what she needed to talk to Dad and me about.

“Well, *that* phone call is one, which might mean something very special is in store for you. It was Dr. Bosh, and he was explaining that they’d be interested in trying a new surgical implant procedure on your eyes if Dad and I were willing to allow it. That would also depend on your desire to have it done. He said that it’s still very new, and there could be no guarantee of how long it would last. What’cha think about that?” I could sense she waited on my response. She always did when this issue arose. I sighed deeply without any desire to give her an answer for or against it. I had been blind for seven years now, and I initially learned to avoid becoming enthusiastic about seeing, again.

If Stevie Wonder, Ray Charles, Jose` Feliciano, and the countless other blind people who survive in this world can and have done it, who am I to change it and be counted among them?

“Mom, I know that it’s your dream to one day have me see you again, but you also have to know that I am fine with it if I don't. For the past seven years, this has been all that I know. I get up every morning and count my way to the bathroom. I run my bath water, brush my teeth, come out and get dressed, and all of this is possible because I've learned how to *live* with my blindness. I know where everything in this house is. I can read. I listen to my radio, and I work at the resale shop. Seeing isn't going to change any of what I've learned as a blind person. Most definitely I'll have the ability to see, but with all that has come about in the years since Helen Keller, seeing isn't as hard as you might think."

She came over and sat on the chair's edge. I reached out and touched her hand. I knew she smiled when I did this and said, "Mom, I sit and hear all that goes on around me. I can't see it in living color, but my mind is able to create for me the same colors that you are capable of enjoying. If I'm happy as I am, please be happy *with* me."

Her hand trembled, and I knew she would be crying, soon. She somehow managed a weak and drawn response.

"You're right sweetie. I was wrong to impose my desires on you. I was overjoyed when Dr. Bosh shared that news, and I got carried away with it. I'm sorry if I upset you or made you feel that you have to do anything regarding your blindness."

I lay my head upon her and said, "Mom, you know that I'd never fault you for wanting a 'whole' child. I'm just trying to protect you in case it doesn't happen that way." She kissed me on the forehead and said, "I know baby. I know." She gets up and walks out of the room. I feel badly that she does not understand my contentment with my condition, but I knew thoughts of maintaining my welfare within their senior years were constantly on her mind.

Another person would not ever want me to have sight as badly as I do, but it had been seven years since I was in the car accident with Aunt Yvonne, Marta, and my little sister, so all I could do was go forth as a blind person without emphasizing new procedures, promising surgeries, or other hope-igniting discoveries.

My head injury left me with what is medically known as Cortical Visual Impairment (CVI). It could be temporary or permanent, and the chances of regaining sight are not made better or worse by either of the instances although head injuries are not the only cause. It is a condition that shows the visual system of the brain does not continuously interpret or understand what's seen by the eyes.

I would be lying if I said I did not sometimes miss being able to watch television or freely walk around without the use of a cane, but this is no longer my reality. I am seventeen now, and I have accepted so much more than they realize.

The Center for The Blind had been very instrumental in shaping me into an independent and determined person. In actuality, there is not too much that I am going to miss out on. I would still be able to go to college, get married, and have children.

I would also be able to work, and I would be as productive as the next person. I was sure Mom would grasp this, and I would be able to see in due time. However, I would not do anything to give her false hope of looking me in the eye again and knowing that I can really *see* her when chances are just as good she will not. I pray she does not believe I am being stubborn or throwing a pit party for myself. Life is grand for me, and I embrace it.

Dinner was a little quieter than normal. Mom and Dad said little, and I could feel the apprehension in the air. When Dad finally cleared his throat, I knew the conversation Mom so eagerly wanted to have was about to take place.

"Janelle, Mom told me that she had the opportunity to share with you that Dr. Bosh had called with information concerning a procedure that could possibly restore your sight. Have you any interest in following through on this to see if you can gain from it?"

I put my fork down and pondered his question thoroughly before answering him.

"Dad, Mom did come in and speak with me, but it wasn't in great detail, and I hadn't thought too much about it to be quite honest. However, I sense that the two of you would like for me to do this, and I don't take issue with it. I guess what I want to know is why you want this for me when I'm fine with the thought that I may never see again?"

There was a gentle stirring from Mom's side of the table as she began to speak.

"Janelle, you are correct when you say that we want this for you, but we want you to understand that we aren't imposing it on you. We only want you to entertain the thought to see what could happen to want to see, again. We do take what you say and how you feel seriously, but do you think that after being given the information and consultations with Dr. Bosh, you might be more interested in it?"

"Mom, I've never ruled out anything totally, but I did make a promise to myself to not keep latching onto false hope, either. What are the specifics of this surgery? What are the chances of my seeing again, and to what degree will I be able to see?"

Mom rose from the table and went into the other room. I was sure she would retrieve the notes she had taken while on the phone with Dr. Bosh. She was very efficient and never left anything to be lost in a conversation. If she had it written down, no one had to wonder about its accuracy. Her work ethic, sense of duty, and overall presence were things that continue to inspire me.

She returned and seemed to have glided into the room. I did not hear her footsteps or other movements of her body. I heard the ruffling paper and could tell she was passing them over to Dad.
They were silent for a moment, probably allowing him the opportunity to read them again before

speaking. I felt his hand touch mine. I smiled and he got started.

"Janelle, this procedure is new, in fact, it's only been performed fifteen times, in Switzerland. According to your mother's notes, it would last four to six hours and you'd be allowed to come home the third day. What the doctors will do is go in, replace a portion of the stem that is responsible for transmitting what you see to your brain. This is believed to be able to help you regain up to seventy-five percent of your sight, based on the condition of your own stem. It appears that the patients who have had this procedure regained their sight immediately, some gradually and some have reported that it's sporadic. It's also been noted that they regained their sight for anywhere from two years to the present time and the first ones were done over four years ago."

I said nothing and continued to sit in silence, wondering if this was all that needed to be said before Mom suddenly spoke: "Well, Janelle, does that sound like something that you'd want to do? We don't want you to rush into it without being comfortable with the information."

I smiled at her and said, "It sounds promising and it seems to be what fifteen people needed, but I don't know if it is something that *I* need to have done. How old were these patients? What was the initial cause of their blindness? How long had they been blind before the surgery was performed?"

I heard the shuffling of the papers again, and I almost burst out laughing. Mom seemed to have known exactly what concerns I might have. She said, "From what I have here, it has the patients listed from ages thirteen to seventy-four. There were six males and nine females to have received these surgeries." Dad was drumming of his fingers, which let me know he was nervous.

"Mom, when are they looking to do this? What needs to be done for us to prepare for it?" I asked.

"Oh Sweetie, if you're *okay* with everything and want to have it done, all I have to do is let Dr. Bosh know, and he will confer with the surgical team that was allowed to observe these procedures and then you will go into sessions with him. It will prepare you for the pros and cons of it," she said.

"*Okay*, why don't you give me a little time to think about this and sort it all out? I'll give you an answer as soon as I can. Is that good?" This time Dad answered.

"Yes, Janelle, we want you to be absolutely sure of it. Take the time that you need."

He patted my hand, and I grabbed it and squeezed it tightly before he can pull it away and said, "Daddy, how much do *you* want me to have it done? How much does it mean to *you* to have me see again?"

There's a gentle shift of his body and in an almost whisper he states, "Nothing would make me happier than to have you go through with this and to know that you'll be able to see me again, but I want you to be happy with it. I want you to be you, whether you're blind or sighted." His voice broke and he walked out of the room.

Mom rose from her seat and came over to me. She sat down next to me and said, "This is going to be hard on all of us and for different reasons. We know that you are an independent girl and are quite ambitious, but I think that there have been times when we have all become comfortable and used to what we want that we don't carefully consider what's good for the other. I'm with Dad as far as wanting you to do this, but I'm going to stand with you on your decision if you choose not to. Okay?" She leaned over and kissed me on the cheek.

"Yes, Mother, it's *okay*. Thank you. I'll have a decision soon, and I appreciate your willingness to let me decide what I believe to be best for me. I'm going to get in bed, now. Do you want help with clearing the table?" I awaited her response before moving.

"No dear, you go on to bed. Sweet dreams," she whispered. I slowly shuffled and felt my way into my room. I went and sat in the chair by the window. I raised it just a little, only wanting to capture the night "music."

I leaned back and closed my eyes to the sound of the crickets, passing cars, and people who were sitting out on their porches. Some were laughing and carrying on like they were the only ones on the block and, others were speaking in a manner for not disturbing those around them.

A slight breeze came in and stirred me from my moment of tranquility. I lowered the window, undressed, and slid into bed. I was sure to turn up the volume on my radio, so the sounds of all of my favorite artists would send me on my way.

Sleep would not come as easily for me tonight for some reason although I had all of the right elements to immediately doze off. I was sure the questions about the surgery and where it would take us was the main reason for it, but it was not the first time I had been faced with whether or not I wanted to go through with one of them.

I tossed and turned like crazy. I rose, sat by the window again, and disappointedly returned to bed. None of it was of any use. Mom was not able to sleep, either. Her light tapping on the door made me aware of that.

"Janelle, are you awake dear?" I sat up and answered, "Yes Mom. Come on in." She eased in and closed the door behind her. I held out my hand, so she knew I wanted her to sit with me on the bed. She started by saying, "I wasn't sleepy and thought I'd drop in to check on you. I'm surprised that you aren't asleep by now though. Are you okay?"

"Yes, Mom, I'm fine. I sat by the window a while. There are times when the sounds of what's going on around me allow me to go to a different place. I can escape and come back as I need to."

"It must be nice to have that mechanism in place. There have been times when I wished I could do something like that, but it never quite happened that way."

The tone of her voice let me know that she had to have been looking past a day and time involving me. I somehow got the feeling it was a 'long ago' kind of sentiment.

"Mother, in *my* world I don't have to try and block out some things. In *my* world, what I hear can be deciphered into many different meanings and relate to me only as I need them to. Being sighted allows me to see and hear those things, but in seeing them, I'm not able to discard them as needed. Once the eyes have taken a photograph and printed a picture to my mind, it's there forever. Words can be misunderstood and played with to make them more acceptable, and that was why I have voiced opposition to seeing, again. I don't know whether it'll be for one month or one year. All I know is that I didn't want to be left in a far worse predicament because of it."

"Janelle, although it has been my desire that you see again, I can look beyond that and focus on that which you deem important to you. It is your decision and we'll stand with you on it. Do what you believe you can live with. It's all going to be *okay*."

She tucked me in and retreated to her and Daddy's bedroom after saying this. I lay there for a while longer. I hated having this decision sitting before me, but it was and I needed to find a happy medium for all of us.

I do not want to necessarily quit before trying, but I would be the only one dealing with the outcome when in the end whether it is good, bad, or indifferent. I guessed I would have an answer for them in the morning. I do not want to prolong this, and I did not want them to keep thinking of strategies or ideas they believe would convince me I needed to do it.

If only my grandmother were still here. She had a special touch, which seemed to make everything vanish without appearing as threatening. She could practically *love* anything, away. I reached into the desk near the bed and grappled around until I found the locket she had given me when I was six years old. I would need it in the morning.

The day started out *okay*. We gathered up the dishes to wash them after breakfast. I turned to Mom and said, "I'm going to go ahead with the surgery." I heard a deep sigh of relief before feeling her hands on my back. She choked back tears and managed a cautious, "Are you sure this is what you want to do?" I smiled in her direction and reasoned, "Yes, if for no other reason than to say that I wasn't afraid to face it head on. Will you please get in touch with Dr. Bosh, and let him know that I'm ready for the pre-op consultation sessions?"

She responded, "Oh yes! Yes, I can do that, now. Are you absolutely sure that you want to do this?" I placed my hands on my hips and looked in her direction while I said, “I can always change my mind, right?”

I laughed to myself as I heard her scurry into the other room and place a call to him. A wave of anxiety hit me, and I steadied myself against the sink. I prayed I would not regret this decision and only time would be able to tell the tale.

I knew she would call Dad next and let him know. He had gone in an extra hour early, so he was unable to leave home with the knowledge he and Mom’s desire (for me to see again) was probably going to happen. I made my way back to my room and sat by the window while waiting for her to come in and share his feelings about it. I barely became settled before she was knocking on the door.

“Come in, Mother.” She entered, sat on the arm of the chair, and started playing in my hair.

“Dad was very happy at the news of your going ahead with the surgery. He said that he’s going to take a half-day, so that he can have a special celebration with you. Is that *okay*?”

I giggled and replied, “I hardly think it’s cause for a half-day of celebration, but I don’t mind.” She started humming, and I lay my head in her lap.

“Jan, Dr. Bosh can get you in, first thing tomorrow. Is that a good time for you? He can push it back if you’d like.” I did not want to answer. I did not want to think about it further at this time, so I pretended I had drifted back off to sleep.

"Jan? Did you hear me, sweetie?" I lay there…nothing. She stood, placed a pillow under my head, and threw a light blanket over me.

The sessions with Dr. Bosh were going by rather fast. It did not seem like I had four sessions already, but I did. They were very informative. He explained everything down to the minor details of what I could expect to happen. Mom and Dad were beside themselves and could not wait until I had given them the official word to proceed and start telling everyone.

Dr. Bosh explained my sight would gradually come back over a few hours after having the surgery. He further explained I should notify him immediately if I started seeing less in one eye than in the other. He said this indicated the surgery had run its course and a more intrusive procedure could be done to allow me more time to have sight.

I was not even going to concern myself with that. I was accepting this for what it was and calling it a day. I had basically made this decision to get Mom and Dad calmed down a bit about asking me to do it.

The night before the procedure, I was sure to eat lightly and not after a certain time. I assured them both it was still something I wanted to do and made a bigger effort to convince myself I would not regret having done it.

A sudden anxiety hit me when they wheeled me away into the operating room, but I was not giving into it. It was too late as far as I was concerned, and I wanted it finished, already.

The surgical team talked to me constantly as they prepped me, and they did a wonderful job of keeping me calm.

"Janelle, I'm Rick Vance, and I'm your anesthesiologist. I'm going to shoot what we call 'Z Juice' into your IV now, and I want you to count back from a hundred for me when I ask you to. Is that good?"

I smiled in his direction and said, "Is fine with me. I don't argue with men who have me hooked up to an IV and is getting ready to shoot something into it." The room erupted in laughter. "Might I add that you also have a wonderful sense of humor?"

I felt a tug here. Then, a tug there and his softened voice finally said, "Okay Janelle, it's all yours. Slowly start counting backwards from a hundred. I need to be sure that they taught you that in kindergarten...errr…or is that college?" I cleared my throat and started in, "One hundred, ninety-nine, ninety-eight, ninety-seven, ninety…"

"Janelle, in just a moment I will begin taking the bandages from your eyes. If you can hear me please nod your head." It was Dr. Bosh's voice, but I was not sure why he was sounding the way that he was. His words were shaky and reminded me of how I would sing into the big box fan that was in one of the windows in my aunt's bedroom.

I realized the surgery was over after collecting my thoughts and nodded, slightly. He began speaking, again, "Now, this procedure wasn't as intrusive [invasive]as some of the other ones, but it was necessary to have your eyes to be disturbed as little as possible for the first six to eight hours after undergoing it. Do you understand that?" I nodded, again. He chuckled and said, "Oh, it's *okay* for you to speak if you wish to. Giving the instruction to nod your head is usually easier than having a patient to speak. What you'll feel will be the surgical scissors that I'll use to cut away the bandage, please remain completely still. *Okay*?"

"*Okay,* Dr. Bosh…when will my parents be able to see me?" He carefully finished the cut, but he does not get to answer before Dad chimes in. "We're right here, baby girl. We're not going anywhere." I smiled. The butterflies that were fluttering about in my stomach seemed to relax and to decrease in number.

"Janelle, I'm going to peel the bandages off now. I do not want you to open your eyes until I have instructed you to do so. Do you understand that?" I nodded again and waited for him to finish. I do not know if it is my imagination or whether this has turned out to be a success, so far. I saw faint beams of light. I gripped the rails of the bed.

"Am I hurting you, Janelle?" I tried to contain myself and answer.

"No Dr. Bosh. I can see small beams of light…and I was a little startled I guess." I hear my parents gasp. Mom started crying and Dad quietly consoled her.

"Well, if you saw streaks of light that's a good sign. Let me clean all of the ointment and drainage from your eyes and we'll see what we've got."

He instructed me to slowly open my eyes as he counted to ten in just a few short minutes after having said this.

"*Okay,* Janelle, can you see my big nose in front of you?" Mom and Dad laughed and cried, simultaneously. A man's silhouette stood before me.

"I can't tell how big your nose is, but I definitely can see your outline. You have a lot of hair on your head? It appears a little bushy to me." We all laughed, and Mom and Dad rushed over to me.

"Oh my goodness! Oh my goodness! Oh my goodness!" was all Mom was able to say as she squeezed the life out of me. Daddy just kept rubbing my face and telling me how much he loved me.

I could only make out their forms too, but they still seemed to be the good-looking couple I remembered from the memories I had before losing my sight.

"Okay folks, I know this is a happy occasion, but I really need to finish up my assessment of the surgery." They stepped to the side through tears and sighs of relief while each of them still held my hands.

"Janelle, the fact that you have been able to distinguish our body images, shapes, etc. is indication that the initial surgery has been a success. However, the next few weeks will be crucial to the continued success of the surgery and future procedures. It's very important that you make me aware of sudden loss of sight, once it has come back to you. You'll need to pay close attention to when it comes and when it acts as if it's going to go. If you are without sight for three days, the nerve and stem cells that were responsible for the overall success of the surgery will shut down and return you to where you were before the surgery. Do you understand that?" I sighed before speaking.

"Yes, basically what you're saying is that you should be made aware of any drastic changes in my sight. If I go for three days without sight, then I'll…I'll…" Mom moved over closer to me and squeezed my hand as she spoke.

"Dr. Bosh, three days without sight will mean that she's back to square one, but does that mean that other procedures will not be possible?" He breathes deeply and responds.

"If she goes for three days without sight, it will greatly reduce the success of another operation. If she goes longer than the three days, I can almost guarantee that it'll be irreversible. That's why any drastic changes should be reported to me ASAP. If it's caught early, the stem can be strengthened, but until a patient has actually regained sight and is relaying marked changes, we can't tell whether or not their sight has the potential to be ongoing."

"Dr. Bosh, I understand all of that and will be sure to keep a journal of what I experience and when I experience it. I want to thank you for all that you've done and no matter what comes about. I'll be thankful for the opportunity to have seen the things around me again."

He approved my departure, and we headed home after I said this. I walked through and experienced sheer elation at the thought of soon being able to see the things that had escaped me for years: the plush, over-sized, floral-print sofa and loveseat; the cherry-wood coat rack positioned behind the door as you enter; and the coffee table adorned with many family pictures, which included me and my youth, were all things I looked forward to seeing again.

I walked through and saw the familiar furniture jutting out at me was beyond words. It was weird being able to see an outline of it and to carefully avoid colliding with it although I had been maneuvering myself around it, forever. I went to my room and placed my bag in the chair that had been a source of comfort for me. I raised the window and smiled as I thought of how I would be able to put pictures with those sounds of my nightly symphonies. Mom came in behind me.

"Jan, why don't I bring your favorite lunch up, and you get a quick nap in, afterwards? How does that sound?" I turned and looked at her. She was still the slender, animated person I remembered. She stood only five feet and two inches in stature and weighed no more than the hundred and thirty-seven pounds she was when I last *saw* her from the looks of it. I cannot wait until I am able to tell her how pretty she looked in the vibrant orange, yellow, peach, lavender and mauve colors that seemed to agree with her.

"Ohhhh! That sounds so good. I'm starving and could sure use it. Following it up with a little nap would be the perfect thing." She left with sentiments of a bubbly-hot, grilled-cheese sandwich, with two slices of tomato and a dill pickle, being in tow.

She made fantastic grilled cheese sandwiches! She allowed the bread to become a golden brown. Then, she added a slice of cheese to each one. She added the slices of tomato after they were nice and melted. The cheese was hot, but the tomatoes were not able to get soft and mushy.

I had already slid into my pajamas and under the covers before she returned.

"Mmmm…That is one, delicious smell. My mouth watered well before you got in here with it," I said.

"Well, you know I've had plenty years to perfect it, so I'm glad that it's still your favorite," she said before she chuckled.

"Mother, I was thinking that rather than writing down any changes that might come about, I could just record them on my cassette player. I mean if

my sight has the potential to be going in and out, I think it would be better to have a means that has always been certain. I won't have to write and can just push the buttons on the recorder and have very detailed and accurate information concerning whatever is going on. What you think?"
She wasted no time speaking.

"I think that's a great idea. No tired fingers and you can do that while sitting up or lying down. So, I'm sure it's a good choice for you."

I tore into the halved sandwich, hungrily. It was so good, and not being allowed to eat past a certain time on the night before the surgery had certainly taken its toll on me. The bread made a soft crunching sound as I sank my teeth into it. The mixture of the melted cheese and cool tomatoes was a perfect combination.

The sourness of the pickle brought the flavor home. Mom was still with me, but it was not until I finished eating that she said anything else.

"Jan, please be sure to record first signs of anything different, *Okay*? I know that you and Dr. Bosh have already covered this, but I wanted you to realize that time can be on your side with this."

I finished the last bite of the pickle and placed the plate on the dresser and said.

"Mother, I intend to stay on top of this. I don't want you or Daddy worrying about that. Just like you trusted me to make my own decision concerning having the surgery, I want you to also trust me to keep accurate records of my progress, *Okay*?"

"Janelle, I'm sure that we get on your nerves sometimes when we are addressing issues with you, but please don't get so angry with us. We really do mean well. You're all that we've got and we just need to know that things are going to be as easy as possible for you as we get older."

I took her hand and rubbed it on my cheek and assured her.

"Mom, I know that. We're going to be fine. I promise"

The next few weeks were wonderful! Daily, it seemed my sight improved, and being able to look at myself in the mirror while combing my hair and getting dressed was something that I missed most. Looking at Dad's handsome face and seeing the joy in his eyes had me on a cloud. He was sure to take me everywhere. We went to the park, the malls, and to the skating rink. We would sit out on the porch at night, so that I could see the evening sky beckoning a twinkling and timid star for a rendezvous.

We were outside upon hearing a loud crash and heard screaming from down the block on one particular night. It startled both of us. He grabbed my arm and attempted to lead me inside. I pulled away from him stating, "Daddy, I can see now. I don't need you to help me inside. What was that? What's going on?"

He stepped out into the yard and jumped back immediately as a dark figure ran past him.

"Get outta the way ol' man!" A youthful male voice shouted as he ran through our yard. I grabbed my chest and screamed out to my father to get back on the porch.

"Help! Help! He took my purse! He took my purse! Stop him! Stop him!" A lady who looked to be in her middle fifties, and who was obviously out of breath, came running down the street.

"Excuse me, did you see which way the boy went?"

My father and I pointed in the direction of the bandit, and she started to go after him, but he stopped her saying, "Miss, you should wait for the police. Don't try to catch him by yourself, it's too dangerous. Did you get a good look at him?"

"Not really…I was getting out of my car and had put my purse on the hood and out of nowhere he came, pushed me down and grabbed my purse. All that I own is in that purse. I have to catch him." Mom came out on the porch with the phone in her hand.

"Here sweetie, it's the police. I heard the commotion and called them. They want to know what's going on." She handed my father the phone and walked over to me.

"I bet that was scary, huh? Are you *okay*?" I was a little shaken by it, but I managed to answer her, anyway.

"Yes Mother, I'm *okay*. Wasn't expecting that I guess, but I'm fine." Everything flickered as I finished that statement. It was like someone had turned a light off and then back on.

The police arrived and filed a report from the lady and my father. They did not have much to go on as far as the description and urged the lady to get on the phone first thing in the morning to call her bank and credit card companies.

Tonight, he would be the one to tuck me in and assure me that all was well. He could tell that it unsettled me a little bit more than I let on.

"Baby girl, when I took your arm tonight it was a natural reaction. I know that you're very independent and can take care of yourself, but what more could I do as a father? It was not meant to make you believe that you're helpless or at the mercy of anyone else. okay?"

I buried my hand in his beard and played with it as I always had. This was our way of easing any feelings of uncertainty. He took my hand and kissed it.

"Daddy, I just want you and Mom to stop worrying about me so much. In actuality, I'm supposed to be worried about you two, but you kill all of that when you worry about me. I'm the product of both of you, so that should tell you something."

He took in a deep breath and said, "You're absolutely right. That is reason enough to know that you are going to amount to much." He kissed me on the forehead and walked out.

I decided I was not as sleepy and went and sat by the window. It was still raised from earlier in the day, so I listened to the midnight sounds and fell asleep contently in the chair.

I called for another follow up visit with Dr. Bosh this morning, so I was glad to get it over and done with. He came in smiling as he had been ever since he knew I was able to see him doing it. He was also very chipper and comical.

"Why, hello there! How are you doing today? Can you tell me what color tie I have on? Is my nose clean? Did I remember to tie my shoelaces this morning? Is that a real lobster climbing the wall over there?"

This was a part of the follow up. I was supposed to look for everything he asked me and make the connection, and he would be able to determine if the strength of my eyes was increasing, decreasing or about the same.

"Hello, Dr. Bosh. Your tie is purple. Your nose is extremely dirty. You have on buckle shoes, and that's not a lobster climbing the wall, but a skunk."

We laughed extra loud this morning, and one of the nurses stuck her head in the door to see what the fuss was about. She cleared her throat and said, "Hey! Hey! You two wanna hold it down? Some of us aren't having as much fun." She smiled and walked out.

He was silent for a few more minutes, and it worried me. I knew why when he spoke.

"Janelle, my tie is green. I bet you knew that and was trying to throw me off, right?"

I mustered a fake little smile and said, "Dr. Bosh, you are a killjoy! You know I knew that tie was green. What? You're the only one who can joke around here?" He pinched my arm and told me next time he would run me through the whole rainbow to be sure.

I guess I should have told him there had been a couple of instances where my sight blinked on and off, or I was able to see out of one eye better than the other.

It could have been caused by stress because I was trying to see all that I could and was giving my eyes very little rest. Nah, I was not going to worry about it. I was going to rest my eyes more though. I hurried out and walked over to the bus stop. Mom was having a hard time with me doing it by myself, but I had to convince her that this was best for me and was a way for me to reach another level of independence.

I still had about twenty minutes before the bus would arrive, so I took out a book and started reading it. It had to be about seven or eight minutes into reading it when I felt a presence beside me. I glanced up and looked into the smudgy face of a little girl. She had long, curly locks of hair that fell well past her shoulders. She would have been an excellent candidate for one of the children's shampoo commercials if it were not so grimy.

She had on a filthy, oversized dress and sandals that looked as though they might have belonged to an older sister. I hadn't noticed anyone with her though.

I didn't want to stare at her too much, so I went back to my reading.

"Do you have anything to eat lady?" I did not look up immediately after she said this, and she pulled on my sleeve to be sure to get my attention.

"Lady, do you have anything to eat?" I placed the book on the seat and turned to look at her.

"Sweetie, who are you out here with?" She turned and pointed towards an old, raggedy, beat up station wagon that was loaded down with what appeared to be clothes and furnishings.

A frail looking woman with matted. short hair was keeping a watchful eye on her and rocking a baby in her arms. I smiled at her and turned my attention back to her daughter.

"I have an apple and some crackers in my book bag, but I can give you some money to take to your mommy, *Okay*?" She smiled and jumped on the seat next to me. The stench was unbearable. She smelled like she had not had a bath since birth. I held my breath as much as I could and gave her a twenty-dollar bill.

I placed it neatly in her little pocket and pinned it with a safety pin. I watched and made sure that she made it all the way back to her mother. Once her mother unfastened her pocket and saw what I had given her, she had the little girl to blow me a kiss.

I smiled to myself, but there really was no reason to smile, period. How was it that this mother and her children were living in their car on the street? The lights went off and came back on, again. This could not have happened at a better time either; the bus was here, and I was about to board it.

Mom had made a nice, crisp salad with all of my favorite ingredients when I made it home. There were raisins, sunflower seeds, black olives, red onion rings, tomatoes, cucumbers, boiled eggs and cheese. It was nice and fresh in addition to the brilliant color scheme, which complimented its presentation. We sat in total silence and enjoyed it. My taste buds were dancing to the rich flavors and textures represented.

The chunks of blue cheese in my salad dressing reminded me of why it so easily became my number one choice. Mom was staring at me in a rather strange way. I wasn't sure if it was real or imagined, but it was enough to make me wonder.

"Janelle, is everything *okay*? You're comfortable with your sight, and the changes that you've had to adapt to aren't you?" I frowned a little, trying to figure out where this was all going. Lately, we have been doing a lot and were enjoying things that had been absent for years. I thought that would be enough to keep questions of my sight off of her mind a while.

"Yes, Mother. Is there any particular reason that you ask?"

"Well, I've seen you shuffle in your steps a little and twice in as many weeks I've seen you run into things. Am I being paranoid or is there something that you aren't telling us?" I forced a chuckle.

"Mother, please stop. I'm fine. You have to realize that I have to get used to seeing again, and it's not as easy as you might imagine. Don't you still bump into things even though you've had sight *all* of your life? Why is it so unheard of for me to do it?"

She did not look convinced of anything that I shared with her and simply said, "I guess it shouldn't be. I just wanted to be sure that you weren't trying to avoid telling us like you wanted to protect us or something."

I did not have the heart to tell her that right now she was a blur to me, or that clear pictures of her had been touch and go for over a week.

"Mom, when things get that way for me, I'll be sure to let you know. I'm aware that you and Dad are going to worry about me regardless, so I won't add to that. Okay?"

She tilted her head to the side and folded her arms across her chest. Whenever she did this, she would also be staring at me in amazement. I smiled and got up and took my dishes into the kitchen.

I went up to my room and flicked on the CD player. At this moment, it seemed to be the only thing that could ease my feelings of uncertainty. Who would have thought that my usual sit by the window would be marred by a couple of teens fighting outside? I shut it and crawled into bed.

It would be the sounds of a new day, which awakened me. The birds were chirping, loudly. Parents and children were moving around noisily, and the constant flow of traffic played the usual street medley. Dad's light tap on the door made me smile as I consented to his entrance.

"Hey Princess, you up yet?" I sat up and leaned against the wall, saying, "Yes I am, handsome. What'cha know good?"

He sat at the end of the bed and rattled off several activities that he wanted me to consider doing after he got off of work. The only thing that sounded halfway decent was our visiting a local art exhibit in town. I let him go on and on, but it was not long before he asked, "Janelle! Is there anything wrong?" I snapped to and replied, "No Daddy, I was just sitting here enjoying your excitement with our being able to do those things, again. The art exhibit sounds good. What time do you want me to be ready?"

"Hmmm…I'm not completely sure. I have to seal a deal with a client tonight, so it would be shortly after that. However, the exhibit starts at 7:00 p.m., so I should be done by that time. If you can be ready, I can zoom by and pick you up. Is that good?"

"That would be perfect. Is Mom going to be joining us?" I asked.

"No, I believe that she'll be having a meeting with the ladies in her community action league. Would you rather wait until later in the week, so that we'd all be able to attend?" he asked.

"Oh no, that's fine. I was just asking."

Seven o'clock came and went. Eight o'clock, nine o'clock, and eventually ten o'clock did the same. I had already showered and slipped into my jammies when he finally made it in

He eased into the doorway of my room.

"I'm sorry, Princess. This joker was playing hard ball to the very end. I wasn't able to sneak away to call you. You forgive me?" I looked towards him and smiled. I was glad that it was night, and he wasn't able to see me struggling to recognize his form.

"That's *Okay*. I know how that can get. We still have a few days." I said.

Our missing the art exhibit tonight bought me time for another day. I could be thinking of something else to do: something that would not require using my sight as much.

"After I get into something more comfy, you wanna go out and sit on the porch with me?" he asked. I perked up and responded immediately. "Yes, I love it when we sit out there and take in the neighborhood and all that surrounds us. I'll be here when you're done."

It did not seem to have taken him long. I had just closed my eyes to wait for him when he was back again, gently shaking me awake.

"*Okay*, Princess, I'm ready. Let's get out there and see what awaits us on the porch of this luxurious establishment." He barely finished before we both burst into a hearty laugh. We went out into the still of the night. It was quite breezy and comfortable for a May evening. I walked a little more slowly with more precise and calculated steps. I hoped would not be paying as much attention as Mom had been.

We laughed and talked about everything from my birth to the present, and it was such a wonderful feeling. He was rather apologetic about missing our date, but I was too pleased to relieve him of any guilt because it was better for me that we had not gone. It would have devastated him to know I was unable explain an intricate design or color scheme if he had he asked me.

Mom came home about an hour after we were out there. She sat with us after Taking off her jacket and shoes. We had not all three sat out here in ages, and it was long overdue. She went inside to make us a light snack, and we continued to talk. For some reason Dad stopped talking in the middle of a sentence and my heart raced.

"Daddy? What's wrong? What were you about to say?"

He placed his hand on me and said, "Princess, everything is fine. Just sit quietly while I take care of this." I heard a male voice speak before I could talk.

"I got this pops, but just in case you get any ideas about testifying for the old bitch up the street, I thought it might be good to remind you that *things* could happen."

My breath was suddenly cut off. I started breathing heavily and put my hands to my chest. I recognized the voice. It was that of the young man who had snatched our neighbor's purse the other week.

"We don't want any trouble, son. Please, just allow my daughter and me to go into the house. I have no quarrel with you or what happened the other night. "

Mom suddenly opened the door and fearing for her safety Daddy jumped up and shouted at her to stay in the house. She dropped the platter that she was carrying our snacks on, and a shot rang out.
I heard her scream, and a blurred someone ran through the yard.

"Baby! Baby! Please say something! Please say something! Can you hear me?" she yelled.
I could hear neighbors running over and trying to assist her. I eased over and hugged the pole of the front porch. I could not do anything. Nothing seemed real to me at this point.

"What about your daughter? Is she *okay*?" someone asked. I heard her coming towards me.

"Oh my God! Janelle! What happened? Are you *okay*? Have you been hurt?"

I said nothing. I rocked back and forth, humming a nursery rhyme that he used to sing to me when I first started school. Sirens from the ambulance and police cars soon invaded the noise of the curious onlookers and people rendering aid to my father.

A police officer pushed passed the crowd and ordered them back from the porch and front yard. They grumbled as they walked away and offered up words of protest.

"Ma'am, I'm Officer Zachary Rhone, can you tell me what happened here tonight? Are you related to the wounded gentleman?"

Mom was searching for words and taking big gulps of air in between each one.

"Yes, he is…umm…was my husband. They were sitting out here while I went in to make us all a snack. When I came out, a young man was here holding a gun. I walked out and must have startled him. My husband jumped up to keep me inside and…and…he…he was shot."

"Who is she to you?" the officer asked, inquiring about me.

"That's my daughter, Janelle. They were out here, together. Maybe you can ask her what she saw and heard before it all happened." He then asked, "How old is she? I'll need you to be present when I question her if she's a minor."

"She's seventeen, and I'm not going anywhere."

He approached me rather, cautiously.

"Hey sweetie. How are you doing? I understand that you were out here and possibly witnessed your father's shooting? Is that true?"

"Ummm…Yes, I did."

"Okay, can you tell me what happened? Take your time, everything's going to be fine," he calmly assured me.

"Well, Mom had just gone in to fix us a snack, and we were still sitting out here talking. All of a sudden he stopped talking, and I got the strangest feeling that he was not okay. When I asked him what was wrong, He let me know that there was a situation to come up. Before I could ask him what it was, I heard him talking to my father."

"Okay sweetie, who is the 'him' that you refer to?" I sighed deeply and responded, "A week or so ago, a neighbor down the street had her purse snatched. My father and I happened to be sitting outside that night, too. The guy who snatched the purse ran through our yard, and my father saw him. He came back tonight warning my father not to testify at his upcoming trial. My mother has already told you the rest. She came out and scared him."

"Well, the good thing is that you've seen him twice and can probably identify him in a line-up. Do you think you can do that?" he asked. I started fidgeting and wanted him to leave, now. I did not want to answer him. Mom came over and sat down beside me.

"I'll be with you baby. You don't have anything to worry about. Do you need a little time?" The warm, salty tears began to flow. I bit my lip and remained as calm as I could.

"Officer, would it be possible for us to do it first thing in the morning? I'm tired and I'm not doing so well right now and I just want to catch up with myself. I need to be by myself for a minute to think it all out. Can I do that?" I asked.

"Yes sweetie, you can do that. We can send a car to pick you and your mother up at about nine in the morning. Will that be good for you?" I shook my head. He asked her for a general description of the person who she saw, and it sounded as though he jotted some quick notes and handed them to her with the understanding we would be making more comments in the morning.

"Come on sweetie, let's get to bed," she said. I rose and bumped into a flowerpot, one that I had very easily maneuvered myself around a few weeks prior. I made it to my room and collapsed onto the bed. She locked up and came in after me. She had not said anything just yet, but I could sense the questions. I patted the bed as our usual sign I wanted her to come and sit with me before she could say anything. I felt the bed sink on the end that she sat on and I reached out for her hand.

She burst out crying immediately and asked, "I was right, wasn't I? You weren't just bumping into things because you were still adjusting. Your sight has been leaving you, and you haven't wanted to say anything. Why Janelle? How could you do this? I thought you wanted to see again." I knew there was no turning back, and I no longer had a reason to be dishonest with her.

"Mom, I know that you may never understand, but I pray that in time you will. Seeing again hasn't been as easy for me as everyone anticipated. It has brought me much pain and heartache."

She stood from the bed and began pacing. Her voice was over here and then over there, as she spoke. "What pain are you talking about? What heartache have you experienced?"

"Mommy, you don't understand. In *my* world, all was well. I didn't have as many worries or concerns. You know I yearned to see the birds fly to and from their nests, but I couldn't handle seeing the dirty and ragged little girl begging for food. I missed seeing the stars at night, but the perpetrators who lurked in the midst ruined that for me, too. Having my sight back also called for me to see all of the ugly things that have been absent from my memory. I know it's silly to you, but having my sight back only to have me regret it wasn't a fair trade, and I didn't have the heart to tell you because I knew how badly you wanted it."

She returned to the bed and asked, "So you're beyond the time that would have allowed you the chance to have another procedure done? Is that what you're telling me?"

I gasped for air as the tears began and said, "Yes Mother, when you saw me stammering and bumping into things, I had already been experiencing drastic changes, but didn't want to share it with you. I had already seen enough. I had already decided that *my* world was the safest for me."

She guided me into her lap, stroking my hair as she asked, "How much can you see? Has it gone totally? I…I don't know what to say. I guess we were wrong. I guess we were unfair and wanted this for *us* without taking into account what *you* needed or wanted. Janelle, you knew you wouldn't be able to identify your father's killer. That's the real reason you wanted to wait until morning, isn't it?"

I could no longer control my emotions. I twisted and turned for several minutes while continuing to cry. I had not experienced a greater anguish since the accident that took my sight.

"Mommy, what good did having sight do for me? My father was gunned down in front of me, and I couldn't identify his killer anymore tonight than I could before the surgery. I should have been sitting out on that porch surgery free. It served the same purpose. When I could have used it most…life had already shown me that it wasn't worth having."

The tears from her face began to land quietly on my face. She held me tighter and rocked back and forth slowly. We both cried non-stop for a countless amount of time and then she asked, "So you're totally blind again?" The lights flicked on and off …then the darkness fell.

Mrs. Breckenridge

"Y'all need to keep those kids in your own darn yard and out of the yards of decent folk, who are trying to keep what they have." Oh, why was not I surprised at hearing "Mrs. B" when she opened her door and yelled that out to me as I headed for the bus stop?

"What have they done now, Mrs. Breckenridge?" I stopped at the end of the driveway and awaited her response. I glanced at my watch and saw I had fifteen minutes before the bus came.

"Look at my yard. They have toys everywhere and over there under them there bushes is some shoes. Don't you know that junk is gone, or do you have so much that you don't miss it?"

"Mrs. Breckenridge, I'll be sure to call once I get to work and have one of the kids come over to pick it up. Thanks *again* for bringing it to my attention." I turned to walk away and she starts in, again.

"Ain't you out here now and see it? That's what I say about you young folks, always in a hurry and ain't going, nowhere. I'll get it myself. I remember a time..." I quickly interrupted her.

"Leave it, Mrs. B! I'll get it!" I sat my briefcase and lunch down in the driveway and headed over to her yard. She stood there with glaring and unmoving eyes. I picked up a few things and glanced at my watch, again. I am going to have to make a mad dash to the bus stop after this little episode. I tossed the things over into our yard, and my eyes ran across something that was not ours as I reached down to pick up a rubber ball. It was breathtakingly beautiful. It was a small pendant with what appeared to be rubies and other stones I did not recognize. I wiped it off and walked over to her. She was still standing in the doorway.

"Mrs. B, Might this be yours?" I handed it to her and noticed the frail little hands and gnarly fingers. I suddenly felt sorry for her. I looked into her empty eyes as she stared at the pendant and squinted as if trying to recall its origin.

"Yes, it's mine, I...I...I don't know how it got out there though..." I made a dash for her. I saw her body was no longer able to remain standing. She collapsed in my arms.

"Mrs. B! Are you *okay*? Mrs. B!" I opened the door with my foot and helped her inside onto the couch. She was pulling away from me and being stubborn about my getting her comfortable on the couch.

"Oh, leave me alone! Don't you have a bus to catch?" This reminded me I left my briefcase and lunch sitting unattended in the driveway.

"Oh shoot!" I ran outside and retrieved them when the bus roared past me.

"Damn!" I said under my breath and returned to check on her.

"Mrs. B, Are you on any medication for anything?" She puckered her lips in a defiant, little manner, and I could tell I was in for a real-long morning. I looked around, found her phone, and called the office.

"Hello Sarah? This is Bridgette, and I'll be taking a half-day. I have an emergency and have some personal family business to take care of this morning."

I saw Mrs. B relax her once-tense posture when I make this statement, and she looked over at me.

"Naw, you go on in to work. I don't need your help." I put my finger up to my lips in an effort to silence her. I hung up and walked over to her.

"I need you to answer my question: Are you currently on medication?" She folded her arms across her chest.

"Mrs. B, I don't have time for this. I need you to answer me so, that we can get you taken care of. Tell me now, or I'm calling an ambulance."

"I ain't on nothing, just been a little under the weather. That's all." I did not believe her, but there was nothing I could do about it. I took inventory of her house and saw it was in disarray, but she was apparently a pack rat, so that was expected.

"Can I call your doctor or son or daughter?"

"Naw, they ain't gone come. They never do." I spun around and asked her who looked after her when she said this.

"I look after myself. Peoples from the church or Senior Meals come by, but other than that, it's just me. I don't need yo' help though, you go on to work, and I'll be fine." I sat next to her and looked at her in disbelief. She turned her head in an effort to hang onto her pride.

"When was the last time you ate a well-rounded meal?" I asked.

"Oh I ate like a horse the other day. I can only take in small meals, though. My stomach ain't like it used to be." I went into her kitchen and determined she was not being truthful. There were no dirty dishes in the sink and no cooked meals in the refrigerator, but I did notice box, upon box, of catered meals just sitting in the refrigerator and some were even on the table. I looked into the cupboards and saw a small amount of canned goods. However, nothing was there to indicate she was eating, regularly. I returned to the living room where she was crying. I rushed over to her.

"Awwww...Mrs. Breckenridge, what's wrong sweetie?" I cradled her in my arms, and the resistance she put up soon faded.

"They threw me away. They don't want me no mo'." I was so shaken; I was barely able to keep my composure. Howevver, I wanted to remain strong for her.

"Who threw you away Mrs. Breckenridge?"

"All of them: my son, my daughter, my grandkids. They threw me, away. They don't understand. I don't mean to be mean and run 'em off."

"Oh, I don't think it's that at all. You know how it is when you get a life of your own and get caught up in what you're doing? Who could throw a sweet, little lady like you, away?"

I saw a smile form upon her trembling lips. I stood, went into her bathroom, and ran some bath water for her. I went into her bedroom, pulled the linen off of the bed, and put on a fresh set. I got her, helped her into the tub, and began to shampoo her hair. I rinsed it gently and smiled to myself because she reminded me of a toddler, enjoying a bath by his mom. Her hair was cottony soft and smelled so sweet.

"Mrs. Breckenridge, I want you to just relax as I get you a bite to eat, *okay*?" I got two more towels, rolled them over, and placed them behind her head. I made sure she was fine before I went into the kitchen to see what I could prepare, really fast. She had tuna, some vegetables, and buttermilk to work with on such short notice. Somehow, I felt she would not mind.

"Bridgette...Bridgette...Sis, it's time to go." I was suddenly jolted back to the present as my sister Melanie spoke to me and helped me realize the graveside service was over. They had begun to clear out. I did not want to remember Mrs. Breckenridge this way. I wanted to remember the peaceful smile that was on her face when I returned to the bathroom to help her into fresh clothes and into a nice, crisp bed. I wanted to remember the bar of soap in her hand with the words "Thank You" scribbled on it. She had done this with the end of her toothbrush. I just wanted to remember her. It was not my wish for her to pass away while she was with me, but I somehow knew it might have been best after meeting her children.

They were cold and distant-acting people. They cried a little, and the son kept looking at his watch like his mother's funeral prevented him from a much more important appointment. It was so sad: she seemed to be a bother to them. Her daughter was gorgeous and was dressed to the nines in what appeared to be a kick-ass Armani suit. She had shoulder-length, highlighted hair and kept squinting as if suffering from a bad headache. She kept a firm hand on a small and oblivious son.

I was walking to the car before I stopped when I heard someone shout, "Miss! Excuse me. Miss!" I turned and saw her son walking towards me.

"Yes, how can I help you?" He extended his hand.

"I'm Jeremy, Mrs. Breckenridge's son. You were the one with her when she passed, weren't you?" I smiled painfully as I remembered.

"Yes, it was me."

"I want to thank you for what you did for her and how you were looking out for her. I live across town and..." I could not take it, anymore. I did not want to hear anymore lies, and I cut him off.

"She knew you loved her. She talked about you all the time. I'm glad that I was there for her." He bristled a little at this and said, "Can I compensate you for her care?" I smiled defiantly and said, "No thank you, she compensated me very well." I pulled the bar of soap out of my purse and showed it to him.

"She was still holding it in her hand when I went in to help her out of the tub. Nothing could be worth more than that." I turned and walked, away. The tears began to flow again, but they were not for Mrs. Breckenridge; they were for me.

Have I Failed You Yet?

"Mommy, what do we do now? Isn't it going to be hard for you to make it now that you and Daddy are divorced?" I smiled at my youngest daughter and tapped her nose with my finger. "No silly. You know I'm not about to let you miss out on anything that you need because your Dad and I are no longer together. I'll have to do what I have to do. I saw my mom do it. She saw her mom do it, and I'm sure that it goes on and on and on, but I'm ready to do it because I have them standing by me as I do it."

She became quiet, and I knew this indicated her mind was at work. I said nothing, yet I waited, patiently. I knew the questions would start. I sneaked a quick peek over at her and laughed inside as I saw the pursed lips and the naturally arched eyebrows coming together as she frowned. She was obviously lost in thought.

"Mommy, am I too young to get a job?" I said as I exploded with laughter. I absolutely lost it at this point and laughed a good laugh. She looked at me in amazement, and I did not dare let her know the laughter on the outside was drowning out the tears on the inside.

I was not crying on the inside because of any real or immediate pain. It was more or less fear. How would we make it now? How would I be able to keep them in a decent neighborhood and used to a life of everything they needed?

I had been with my husband for eleven years and married to him nine of those years. He was a good man and took care of home for many years before the trouble started. I cannot even recall when the trouble started, but I remember going into a mode that I had never experienced before when it did. Nothing seemed to matter, and I was virtually without emotion. I do not remember crying or being upset about a lot of things.

I always tried to speak of their Dad in a decent manner, regardless of what happened. He was not my oldest daughter's biological father, but you could not tell. He came in and certainly filled the shoes as her "father."

I remembered times when I was extremely jealous because she became so close to him; it seemed to place me on the back burner. He would take her to basketball games and other little outings, which left me feeling trapped and unable to break free of my "housewife" role.

We would laugh to ourselves when people said she must have gotten her height from him or some other characteristic they imagined. I learned to love it because he had been a wonderful father and the best husband he could have known.

In fact, as I sat back and recalled the number of uncles, cousins, and friends of his who were "layin' 'em and playin' 'em." Was it any wonder he thought this was the norm? Nevertheless, this was a guilty man's argument with little or no room left for negotiating.

As You Like It

You did all you could to make your own marriage successful when you came from a broken home. Unfortunately, this was not always feasible. My heart and mind were clear with believing I did all I could to make it work.

The trouble...hmmm, when did this begin? I shuffled through my recollection, shifted, and turned as I tried to rattle it loose. I had to say the trouble began when he started hanging with his single friends.

I allowed him his freedom and did not have a lot to say to him, but damn, enough is enough. I got tired of him dragging in at all hours of the night and having little or no remorse at my being up most of the night wondering if his butt was alright. I was sick and tired of the nonsense, and my threats of leaving fell upon deaf ears. Brother was so sure I would not be willing to leave to fend for our daughters, alone. Yeah *okay*.

He was right on that count, but you should trust me when I say the strength crept up on you. We separated twice for an extended period of time, and I wore out a pair of kneecaps asking God for endurance.

Finally, the day came when my marriage would be dissolved, and I would be sitting in the dark and crying. I do not know if I cried tears of joy, sorrow, or all of the above. I was scared and did not know what to expect. I would also raise two children, alone now.

Motherhood itself did not scare me, but the thought of keeping adequate employment, decent living conditions, and a firm hold on the girls was suddenly beginning to terrify me.

One thing I knew for sure was I refused to let loneliness and desperation find its way into my otherwise wholesome existence. I had not been alone for many years and visions of waking up and reaching for "him" often times played in my head.

"Girl, you have too much going for you to believe that you have to jump up in a relationship with a man. You can do bad by yourself." I let this repeat itself in my head like my girlfriend had just said it or something. I knew she was right, and I knew I had to live a life for the sake of my girls that was good for them.

The older one came to me many times after the divorce and said, "Mommy, don't get married again until I am grown and out of the house. I don't want to do this, again." I did not know whether to laugh or cry at her remark since neither of them seemed appropriate.

Sure, I would date and things, but it did not do much good because I would always manage to push a man away when I thought he was getting too serious. It did not help if I thought I liked him too much, either. I would cleverly start a fight and see him on his way...for good.

The killing thing is that I never really knew I was doing this until my sister pointed it out.

"You're going to be old and miserable because every good man who comes along and expresses an interest in you, you find a way to run him off."

What the hell did she know? She was not one to deal with men too long either, so her telling me this was like a pimp telling a drug dealer not to peddle his wares. You know what I mean?

Nevertheless, life went on, and I had to take it one day at a time. Do I want to do it, alone? Not necessarily, but if it meant peace of mind, a sense of security, and a time of nurturing and bonding for me and my girls...so be it. I took my little one into my arms. I played the words back and forth in my head before using them on her.

"Baby girl, you know when I told you that just because Daddy and I aren't married anymore that you'd still be *okay* and able to have both of us in your life?"

She began to squirm, as the thought still was not a pleasant one for her. "Yes mommy I do." I took her face in my hands and have her to look at me.

"Then know that you're going to be fine. Dad and I have moved away from each other, but you and your sister will *always* be the center of our world. Do you understand that?"

The puzzled look on her face said it all, but I know her, so I knew that she was going to respond in a way that she thought I needed to hear.

"Yes mommy I do." I smiled at her and kissed her on the nose.

"Good, then also know that whatever it takes for you and your sister to be safe and able to handle things, I'm willing to do. If you ever have a time or two when you're left wondering what's going on, just ask and I'll be happy to explain why things might seem different."

She jumped up out of my arms before I knew it.

"*Okay* mommy, can I go watch TV, now? My favorite cartoon is coming on." I winked at her and waved my hand to dismiss her. She blew me a kiss and started out of the room.

"Baby girl," I called out to her and waited before she peeked back around the door into the den.

"Yes mommy?" I hesitated for a moment, not knowing whether she would be able to comprehend what I was about to say. However, I wanted to say it just the same.

"Have I failed you yet?" She giggled and said, "Oh Mommy, now you're being silly." She turned and ran down the hallway. I closed my eyes and smiled to myself because *that* let me know we would be fine.

Will You Watch Me Die?

"What kind of sick joke is this?" I screamed into the phone after hearing those words spoken to me. I sat down on the sofa and waited for a response even though I knew I should have hung up.

"Miss? Is this Miss Crenshaw? Who used to work at Colonial High School?" I sat up at attention this time, and my heart skipped a beat. Who was this who had called me after so many years of being gone from that place? Being a teacher at Colonial High School had been one of my less-than-happy endeavors. The principal was a megalomaniac with no sense of time, place, or being, and I wanted to continue to keep it in the past. Who was this coming back to haunt me after all of this time?

"Who might you be, and why do you ask?" The voice on the other end chuckled and said, "I see you still have that snappy mouth and can still handle your own. That's what I always liked about you." I did get a sense of familiarity when he said this, but I still was not quite sure I knew who he was.

"We aren't getting anywhere with the verbal gymnastics. Can you please tell me who you are and why you've called?" There was a long pause, and then he spoke again.

"Miss…This is Renaldo. I was in a few of your classes about ten years ago at Colonial, and I wanted to call to..." at hearing him say his name, my heart sprang into its inquisitive mode and I burst out immediately, “Naldo! How have you been? It’s been a while. What are you doing for yourself these days?” He cleared his throat.

“Miss, didn’t you hear what I asked you when I called?”

I went back to the beginning of the phone call to retrieve any statements he made, and I was suddenly confused, and a feeling of dread enveloped me when I realized how the conversation began.

“Yes, you asked me if I would watch you die. What does that mean? Why would you ask me something like that? I was always onto you about your sick sense of humor.” I tried a nervous, little laughter to ease the tension, but, I knew in the pit of my stomach what Naldo was going to share with me would have me doing anything but laughing.

“Miss, I got into a little trouble a few years ago, and my time has come...I need you to watch me die.”

“Naldo! Stop this now! What are you talking about? I’m going to hang up now because I will not do this with you!” I slammed the phone down and tried to stop the swirling sensation that had taken my head hostage and tossed it about like volleyball.

I stood and paced the floor as I recalled the memories of this tall, skinny, and mouthy kid who gave me much grief that year at Colonial. Renaldo Barnes was a young man from a broken home who had to fend for himself, his little brother, and sister while his mother led a lifestyle that defied the laws of common decency and motherhood.

How could he be calling me now with something like this? What was he thinking? *Renaldo Barnes?* I sat at my desk, waiting for his response before I marked him absent. I looked around the room and saw that no one was going to answer. As I went to mark him absent, he slid through the door of the classroom.

"Have you called me yet Miss, I'm Naldo Barnes?"

"As a matter of fact, I just did and you're tardy." He stirred a little.

"Do you have a pink slip?"

"Awww, man! Come on now! If you just called me and you didn't have the chance to mark it yet, why can't you say that I'm here? One more tardy and I have to do after school detention, and I will lose my job."

I had made it up in my mind to make an example of him, so the kids would not think I was a pushover, but something about his plea was genuine. I made an example out of him; however, he had the benefit of the doubt resting in his favor.

"Look, it's your job to do what you have to do to get here on time and deal with the consequences if you're not. I'll give you another chance, but after that, you're on your own. Take your seat, please." He winked at me suggesting he knew I was bluffing, and I would see how determined he was to challenge me as the school year progressed, accordingly.

I smiled as I remembered all of the fights I had broken up, and I smiled as I remembered the times I had jacked him up in the hallways for misbehaving. My heart did not want me to believe that this kid, who was now calling me to ask me to watch him die, was the same young man, not *my* Naldo.

Naldo was a three-time loser. He was the oldest of three children by three different fathers. His mother was a drug addict/prostitute who beat them unmercifully and left for days at a time without them knowing her location. He was also a poor, black youth who was born in one of the roughest of neighborhoods in Oklahoma City. His only inspiration came from watching war movies and wanting to be a fighter pilot.

One might be led to believe he did not possess that type of material at first glance. However, I would come to unlock the mind of a genius. Naldo was a walking encyclopedia. He could blurt out statistics and statements capable of keeping me awake throughout the night in an attempt to dispute them.

He also had an easily abated, violent streak for those taking the time to understand his reason for it. He had a smile that lit up the room and a heart of gold. His younger sister and brother were his pride and joy, and he took care of them better than any adult could.

He kept them neat and clean in such a way; their appearances would not reveal their absence of a decent family or a promising role model at home. His little sister Kaneisha was always neatly dressed, and his female friends from class kept her hairdo up to par. She would have her braids, ponytails, and waves rocking. Everyone who knew of their personal agony kept it to himself or herself.

Naldo's mother was an only child, and she had broken her ties with her parents after disapproving of her relationship with his father. She left home and never attempted to contact them after becoming pregnant with Naldo. Obviously, he split before Naldo was born and left her to fend for herself in an already messed up world.

She became adjusted to entertaining older men and whatever she thought she could do to keep Naldo in diapers and shelter. Her mind was one of promise and greatness as well, so there was no wonder he got it from her. She was in her junior year at Fountain View College, in upstate New York, when she met Richard and fell head over heels in love with him. She was on the honor roll and had a life of easy times ahead of her.

He got her strung out on dope and abused her, continuously. Her academics and everything spiraled downward after that. She cared about nothing or no one. She stopped attending classes, and the institute forcefully removed her from their grounds. Months passed before her parents ever saw her and learned what really happened.

They denounced Richard and saw her for the last time without ever knowing the gender of the grandchild she was carrying. Oh, why did I hang up on him? What if he was serious? How did he get my number? I have not ever been listed in the phone book. For heaven's sake, it was ten years ago that I last had him in class. Where had he been, and what had he been doing?

I rushed into my room and started frantically searching through the papers in one of my drawers. Something came to mind, and I thought it might explain the situation to clarify it for me. Where was it? Why did I not remember where I had put it? I ran across credit card bills, utility bills, and all other things. Why was I not finding it! There it was! It was neatly tucked away in the left corner with papers I had so meticulously stacked. I saw one letter from one J. H. Bell, Attorney at Law. I opened it and began to read it. It was a wonder I could make out any of it since I was shaking terribly and still rather disoriented at the news. Nonetheless, I began to read it, anyway:

Miss Crenshaw,

I'm acting on behalf of my client Renaldo J. Barnes. I represented him in a murder case eight years ago, and he has lost an appeal to have a new trial. His death sentence will stand, and he is scheduled for execution on October 17th of this year.

He is able to have witnesses present and has asked that I find you in an attempt to see if you would be there for him one last time. I know this may come as a shock to you, and I'm sorry for bringing this to you in such an informal manner, but he has spoken very highly of you, and wanted you to know that you made the difference for him when he was in school.

If you'd be as kind as to notify me of your decision, I can start working out all of the details to assure him that his last wishes will be carried out. Feel free to call me at the numbers listed or you can respond to the address provided. I would like to answer any questions or concerns that you may have.

Sincerely,
J. H. Bell

"Noooooo!" I screamed out loud in the empty room. This could not be happening. Not *my* Naldo. It was not right; it was not fair. Surely, God did not let him make that complete change to die a statistic in the penal system. I walked back and forth and tried to shake the thoughts of his upbringing from my mind.

I sat on the bed and laughed uncontrollably when I remembered how he had convinced the class I had quit. I saw the surprised looks on their faces when I walked into the room the next morning although I was late. I was sure he made it seem real.

My laughter soon turned to coughing and heaving. It was so severe; it made me strike out to the restroom. I collapsed over the sink and seemingly vomited for about ten minutes it seemed. I wanted to wake up. I wanted this horrible nightmare to end. I wanted Naldo to be back in my classroom, again. I washed my face and returned the bedroom to lie down. The phone rang, and I grabbed it before it could ring again.

"Hello?" It was him. "Miss, I'm sorry that you thought I was playing with you. I really am going to die, and I wanted you to be able to see me one more time. I thought my lawyer sent you this information, but I guess he hasn't done it yet."

I cleared my throat of any sadness and tried to sound optimistic for him.

"Yes, Naldo, he did get that to me quite a while back, but I hadn't found the time to respond yet. Please, understand that I wouldn't be able to do that though. I can't be a witness for you. I wouldn't be able to...to..."

"Go ahead, say it, Miss. I'm okay with it. I know that I'm going to die. I know a lot of things because you took the time to show me, and that's why I can live with what I've done and the price I have to pay, now."

"Naldo please, I'm so glad that I could be there for you, but I don't think I could do that. Please, don't ask me to do that."

There was a long moment of silence and then he spoke.

"I understand, Miss. I was just asking since they can't find my moms. I can't ask my sister and brother to see me like that, but I knew that if I could find you, I might have a prayer. Thank you for not hanging up on me this time. I won't call you, again. I appreciate all that you were to me and how you got me started on the right path. Please, don't be disappointed because I strayed and ended up where they said I would, anyway."

I bit my lip and touched my chest to make sure that my heart would stay there. The tears welled in my eyes, and I stifled the sobs, which were rising in me.

"Naldo, I could never be disappointed with you. You're a remarkable young man, and I've always admired the way that you stepped up to the plate to be the father figure that your younger brother and sister needed. Having you in class made me a better person, too. It helped me to be more patient, trusting, and willing to step outside of my world to see what it might be like in someone else's, and I want to thank you for that."

He laughed, lightly "I know I was bad. You don't have to try and say something nice because I'm dying. I'm ready to pay for what I did. God has put some very sincere brothers in my life and I'm ready."

I covered the phone with my hand and cried silently for a few minutes.

"I'm sorry about that. I thought there might be someone at the door."

"No you didn't, Miss. You were crying. Don't feel sorry for me. I really am fine, and I want you to be okay." I was angry with him, now. He always knew me so well and knew how to play me.

"Yes Naldo, I was crying. I don't know what to say or what to think. When they transferred you to the new school, I thought you might be *okay* and would be able to thrive since you'd be away from some of the kids who I thought weren't so good for you to hang around with. What happened? Are you able to tell me? Have you exhausted all of your appeals?"

"Yes, there are no more appeals available to me, and I did do it, Miss. That's all that counts, now."

"What did you do? I mean how could it have come to this?" He sighed and I followed along as he began to speak.

"My little sister started dating this guy who I thought was pretty cool at first. When she started coming home with black eyes and swollen lips, that all changed. Miss…My moms got beat by men. She beat us in return. I wasn't going to let my baby girl go through it, too...I couldn't."

"Naldo, was he the person you killed?"

"Yes. He beat her so bad one night that he put her in the hospital."

"The police didn't care and didn't do anything, so I had to make him pay for all the hurt and pain he caused my sister. Miss, you know Kaneisha was sweet and didn't deserve that." I smiled as I saw her bangs flowing in the wind as she'd run to him after school.

"She was. How are she and Darrell doing?"

"Darrell is in the service. He likes it and wants to make a career out of it. Neisha is a nurse and lives in St. Louis with a friend of hers she met in nursing school. Now, you see why I can't ask them to see me like this?" I understood and felt his pride for them.

"They have gone on to be something real good and positive. They don't need this. I talk to them all the time, and they know that I'm going to die, but I didn't want them to actually see it. " I agreed. Although my heart was now shattered, I managed a smile as I thought about how well things had turned out for them. I was so relieved that they hadn't returned to that cycle of abuse that was so prevalent in their lives.

Darrell was not a streetwise thug who had no hope or aspirations. Neisha was not promiscuous and bed hopping in an effort to "find" love.

"Miss…Is your 'no' a strong 'no' or will you think about it?"

Hearing this motivated me to put my fear aside, and I agreed to find the strength to come watch him die. I asked him to pass my phone number along to his sister and brother, so I could have contact with them if it was necessary.

My heart was not as heavy because he was quite mature when I ended my call with him this time, and the peace within him had shone through. I called his attorney and told him to do whatever was necessary for me to see Naldo off.

October 17th rolled around faster than I wanted it to. It was two months ago from the time we had talked, and it just did not seem possible I was sitting here at the prison gates, waiting for entry to watch him die. I wore a beige dress with a ruffled bottom. I pulled my hair up into a tight bun and let a few strands fall to the side and back.

It was strange because I did not know what would be appropriate or how I should dress, but I did know I would not be wearing a depressing black or blue ensemble. I wanted something a little warmer and comforting.

I was led into a small dark room where reporters, prison officials, and members of the victim's family were seated after being searched, fondled, and instructed out the nose. A big window with drawn curtains was in front of us.

I hesitated about where to sit because I did not know what to expect. I looked around and saw a few people consoling one another. Reporters were taking notes, glancing at their watches, and preparing to file their stories, undoubtedly.

Finally, the curtains were opened and guards were leading him into the room. He was shackled at his hands and feet, which caused him to do a penguin like shuffle when he walked. It reminded me of the time he was trying to teach me one of his crazy dances. He looked out into the room, and he let out the smile when his eyes met mine, which had been such a constant in my room that year.

I smiled back at him. He raised his hand and waved. I was a little shocked at this display by him, but I was no longer troubled by it after realizing that he had made peace with himself.

I looked him over and smiled. His young, handsome face looked the same. His body was more defined, and it was obvious weightlifting had done him a world of good. His facial hair was very neatly trimmed and complimented the deeply chiseled eyes that were always taking in all of his surroundings without allowing anything within him to escape unless he allowed it.

They laid him on a gurney that had straps to secure him at the waist, legs, chest, and wrists. He looked out at me the whole time they worked on him. I smiled and hoped this would be quick and painless for both of us, mainly him.

A man who resembled a doctor walked over and started an IV in his hand after strapping him in. I turned my head when the blood ran down his hand from the insertion of the needle. I looked back, and he winked and smiled, again. A different man came over and injected something into the bag, which held the fluid that would seep into his veins.

The prison warden motioned to a guard who then hit a switch and began to speak.

"Ladies and gentlemen in the witness room, Mr. Renaldo Barnes will be addressing you at this time. He'll speak and then we'll carry out his sentence of death by lethal injection. We ask that you remain seated until a time of death has been noted. We thank you for your cooperation."

My right leg began to tremble, slightly. The sign was so evident when something troubled me. I was glad that it was not noticeable to anyone else. Naldo cleared his throat and looked towards the family of the young man he killed.

"I'd like to ask you all to forgive me for taking something so precious to you away from you. I know that you might not be able to find it in your hearts right now, but I hope that before it's your time to leave this place...you will." They sat emotionless, and they did not blink an eye. He looked at an older man who was directly in front of him in the witness room.

"Marvin, thank you for all that you've done, the strength you helped me find, and the love you showed me in the form of the father I never knew. Know that all that you shared with me wasn't in vain."

The man smiled as tears streamed down his face. I bit my lip when he turned towards me. I already knew I would not make it through this.

"Miss Crenshaw, you caught me at a time when I was falling and you made me do better. You never judged me and found good in me no matter what. I carried that with me everywhere that I went, but when I could have used it most..." His voice trailed off, and I crossed my arms in front of my stomach to muffle the sounds that were coming from it.

"Thank you for your love and support. Please, keep in touch with my little brother and sister. May God bless and keep you all." He looked at the warden.

"I'm ready," and the warden looked at the doctor who started the IV. He retrieved a syringe, which was laid on the table and injected its contents into the tube at the wrist of Naldo.

I felt myself rocking back and forth at this point, and I no longer cared there were others in there with me. Naldo coughed a little and looked out at me, again. He managed a very weak smile and raised his other hand in a farewell gesture. He took a deep breath, and no others followed it.

The warden stepped forward, had the doctor confirm his time of death, repeated it to the witnesses, and dismissed us just like that.

I really failed to remember how I made it home since I cannot even recall starting the car. I entered my home, slumped on the bed, and cried for what seemed like hours. I walked into my bathroom and ran some bath water after pulling myself, together. I noticed the message light blinking on the answering machine when I came out and suddenly remembered I had not checked the mail or anything else since arriving home. I sat on the edge of the bed and played the message.

"Miss, I want to thank you for seeing me off, today. You gave me hope in high school, and you've given me hope, now." I trembled and continued listening.

"I know that I was stubborn and rowdy in school, but I want you to know that I knew that you had my best interest at heart. You were what I wished my mom could have been. Thank you and I hope to see you, again. I love you."

I rewound the message and played it, repeatedly. He had the audacity to believe he knew me so well to leave this message on the machine while I was in route to witness his execution? I found myself smiling again because it was evident he had made this connection with me and knew what I held in my heart and mind.

I never perceived life in the same way after that, either. I lived every moment to the fullest and tried to let each and every one of my students know they had a special place in life, society, and the great hereafter.

I still played Naldo's last message to me. I do not cry when I listen to it, now. I smiled and thanked him for strengthening me. It was funny for us to believe we held all of the answers in our minds as teachers. Unknowingly, some of them escaped from us, and we, in turn, could become the students.

Aunt Von, I Hope You Can Read This

I had learned the early morning phone call was no longer dreaded. Today, I was shown how common it could be to get a call bearing bad news at any hour. I was working on the last few pages of my book when the phone rang. My daughter Adjonae` (Ad-jun-ay) answered it and turned to me with an inquisitive look.

"It's Tina?" I sat for a moment and tried to recall a "Tina."

"I don't know a Tina. It's probably a bill collector, but give it to me, anyway." I prepared myself for the usual spiel of a bill collector and was surprised that it turned out to be my nephew's mom. Surely, you were wondering why I would not know her by name and, trust me, it could easily be explained, but that was a whole, new story. She began to ask me about the last time I spoke with my Aunt Yvonne in New Jersey, and I was not slightly interested in the conversation. I was more concerned as to why she was asking me this. I heard someone in the background and asked her who it was.

She told me it was my sister Angel. I no longer wanted to talk to her and ordered her to put Angel on the phone. Angel accepted the phone, and I asked her what Tina was talking about. I was not prepared for what she had to tell me and she simply repeated one thing.

“Call mother and let her talk to you.” I was all too familiar with this little run-around and said, “No! You tell me what is going on.” She stated, “I don’t know everything, and that’s why mother told me to tell you to call her.”

“Are you lying to me? You need to tell me before I call her.” I demanded. “No, I’m not lying and it’s not that anyone has died or anything.” This gave me a bit of relief since they never spoke to me about sorrowful things if I were home, alone. I called my mother, and she also asked about the last time I spoke to Aunt Von.

“Mother, why are you asking me this? Why do you need to know all of that? What’s wrong?” I heard that little reluctant sigh of hers, and I rocked nervously as she began.

“Aunt Von is sick again, and she’s at Petra’s. I was wondering had anyone told you yet. Call Petra and get the full details of what has come up this time.”

I sat there dumbfounded and somewhat indignant at what I was hearing.

“Sick again? What are you talking about?” Her voice quivered a bit, but I managed to hear “The cancer is in her liver and both breasts now.” I could say no more. I sat there in suspended animation as tears ran freely down my cheeks. Adjonae` stood in front of me pleading to be told of what had me so distressed. I motioned for her to hold on and sit down a minute.

As You Like It

My Aunt Von and I are extremely close. I lived with her three times in my lifetime. The first time was when I met Adjonae's Dad (while visiting her in New Jersey), and the other times would be for sheer love of the woman. I returned there after my husband and I separated and attempted to reconcile one of the other times.

He was living in New Jersey with his parents, and the rest of us were in limbo. I had made up my mind we were going to "crap or get off the pot." I was tired, and we were going to have some form of closure.

Unbeknownst to me, my aunt and her husband had been separated, and she was having a rough time with things herself.

It was a total surprise to me when I got there and learned of this, but I never let her know how much it saddened me.

My cousin Petra had moved back home to help her out, and I made sure I put my change in the pool as soon as I started working and had active child support. We grew closer and loved sitting up late at night from chatting upon arriving from work.

My aunt was a nurse, and she worked the eleven-to-seven shift at a nursing home. I was an insomniac, and I spent much time watching television when she entered the residence. Those late night chats and laughs drew us closer than anyone possibly ever imagine.

My cousin Petra was home a lot and we grew closer too, but there was something about that heffa,

Aunt Von. I guessed because she was so nonjudgmental and had a way of supporting your butt at all costs.

It was obvious to everyone we were close and shared a bond that was like no other. I was born and raised in Oklahoma City, Oklahoma away from all of my blood aunts.

Our aunts became my mother's closest friends from church. The only time I saw my aunts were at family reunions or funerals, so there was no other "connection" to them. My mother had two brothers who lived in Oklahoma City. We did get to see them a little more often.

"Shandra, are you there?" I was so far gone in thoughts of Aunt Von that I had forgotten that I was on the phone with mom.

"Yes, I'm still here, so what are you saying?" She was getting annoyed with me at this time, and I knew it was not because of me. Nevertheless, it was because she did not like knowing I was in any type of pain. What made it worse was I was in Texas, and she was in Oklahoma and could not be of any other assistance to me.

"Call your cousin Petra and let her explain everything to you and call me back." I just broke down and cried at this point, and I did not know what to do.

"Is she coming home? Will I need to go get her?" I asked.

"Shandra, I don't know. She's trying to get her disability and things situated, so that she can have everything in place when she does move."

I sat and cried because I knew this was not good for her to hear either, but I did not know what else to do. I did not know what else to say. I did not know what else to think.

"I don't have Petra's number. I had it, but I misplaced it and would have to tear up the house looking for it." She sighed heavily as she wanted to hurry and get off with me and not hear my anguish.

"Well, let me get it and call you back. You know I have to get off of here, now." I nodded as if she could see me and ended the call with her. Adjonae` rushed at me before I knew it.

"Mommy what happened?" She was already in tears and anticipating some type of "bad" news.

"Aúnt Von's cancer has spread to her liver and both of her breasts, now." I looked at her as she collapsed on the couch and cried uncontrollably. She loved some Aunt Von, too. I gave her *Yvonne* as her middle name, and I was glad that I had at this moment. I wanted a forever reminder of my favorite aunt.

Aunt Von's granddaughter and Adjonae had given us migraines like crazy, and that was another way that she and Adjonae` secured such a loving bond. She had watched them on occasion while Petra and I went clubbing back in the day, so she had her hands full.

The three years we lived with Aunt Von were wonderful yet bittersweet. The sheer fact I was with her meant more and outweighed the negative. I remember one Thanksgiving when she had a friend to cook a fried turkey. I had heard about them, but I had never tasted one. He dropped it off and we "sampled" it throughout the night. Obviously, we had nothing but vegetables for our little Thanksgiving feast by the time our sampling was finished. We laughed a while about that one.

I wondered if I could find the strength to want to finish my book as I sat in the chair and stared at the computer. I grabbed the phone and called my sister. I lit into her before I knew it when she answered.

"How could you let someone else call me and tell me something like that?" I could hear her stumbling for words and continued my barrage of questioning.

"Why didn't you tell me what she was going to say to me? I don't know her, and you sat there while she told me about my aunt!"

"Listen, mother told me to call you and tell you that she wanted you to call. It wasn't my choice; I was doing what she asked me to do."

"NO! You could have told me before I talked to her, so that I'd know what to expect and to be prepared for what she had to say to me. I don't know Tina like that and for you to let her relay a message like that to me was wrong!"

"Look, I didn't tell you for this very reason. We don't know who is at home with you, and I didn't want to have you all upset and unable to handle this. Who's at home with you?"

"Nae-Nae is here with me. Bianca is gone and don't you ever let an outsider call me and tell me something like that!" I could hear the defeat in her voice as she agreed to have Mom call me with my cousin's number and that was that.

I walked and paced repeatedly, and I was totally unaware that Adjonae` was watching me and obviously distressed at my reaction to this news. She took the phone and eased out onto the porch with it. A few minutes later Bianca called and told me that she was on the way home. I looked over at Adjonae`, and she looked away as if denying it was not coincidental Bianca had called. I sat and looked at the screen to my computer and cried. What else was there to do?

I had no way to reach my aunt until I found Petra's number, and I called my aunt's number and left the message for someone to call, despite not knowing how soon the messages would be checked on the answering machine.

"Lord I know I have no right to ask you for anything, but if you take her, please don't let it be while she's so far from home." I cried this, over and over again. I remember pulling on my hair so much that it made my head sore. I cried until I was physically weak. Bianca came in a short while later and stared at me, helplessly.

"Mommy, go ahead and cry and get it out. You don't need to get sick. Are you *okay*?" I said nothing to her as I knew the tears were on their way. I simply buried my face in my hands and cried, silently.

Aunt Von,

I do not know where we go from here or the outcome's result. All I know was that I love you and was able to endure all that I did because your strength radiated so brilliantly towards me. I remember your teasing me about wanting me as a child and how you allowed Mom and Dad to get halfway up the road (while leaving a family reunion) and then you reluctantly flagged them down to show them that they were one child short.

Excuse me while I laugh here

You might not have gotten me at that young age, but you made up for it when I did finally make it to you. No one could ever take the place of mommy, but if someone had to, it would be you. I had seen you go through some times that would have shaken many women (Mommy excluded, of course, lol), and it helped me to roll with the punches when life dealt me some crazy hands. What possible way was there for a niece to show her favorite aunt how much she loved and appreciated her? I did not know, but no doubt existed I would still be searching.

As You Like It

Aunt Von, I hope you can read this...

*My aunt would not live to see this story in print as she passed away on November 16, 2002 at 7:45 a.m. I had decided to go and read this to her, but it was not meant for me to see her until she was ready for her trip back home. I arrived in New Jersey during the same day she passed. Then, I realized it was meant for me to be a source of strength for her daughter, my "sister," Petra, who *never* left her bedside. I had never seen strength like I had seen in Darrell (Petra's brother and my cousin) who came up from North Carolina to make this transition a smooth one. Aunt Von, I *knew* you read this. Maybe, you did not do it with your eyes, but you read it with your heart and mind as you clung to life and waited to know I would be there to take care of your baby girl, again.

Rest well,
I love you. *

Big Momma's Porch

"I know I don't hear mouths in there talkin' and ackin' a fool while the Lawd is doin' his work."

We all stopped giggling and talking immediately when Big Mama said this. She was a tall, proud, and "no nonsense" type of person, one who you just did not take the chance of catching a good switching from.

"Ummm...no, Big Mama…that was Daniel... he…he was coughing."

The thumping and crackling of the storm that was going on outside still had not been enough to keep her all-too hearing ears from zeroing in on our mischief. She had always made us be quiet during storms for as long as I can remember.

"God is talking to us for a reason, and when HE does, we need to stop er'thang and hear HIM out. If you be still long enough, you can know exactly what it is HE'S saying."

"*Okay*, Big Mama…we know." We knew it was okay to start up again when we heard her hummin' her favorite church song. Paul rolled over, faced me, and said, "Ruthie, you sho' be lyin' yo' butt off!" All five of us covered our mouths with our hands and laughed into them. I was always quick on my feet and needed to keep as much distance between Big Mama and myself as possible.

If she had entered, started snatching up bodies, and beating them with those switches that she picked out once a week mind you, which promised pain….

We were visiting her for a couple weeks this summer, and we knew what was in store for us: a lot of chores, "sit up straight," and sideways glances. I think she was the only person who is able to keep us all in check.

She was the oldest of fourteen children. Three of them died in infancy, and she learned very early how to be a 'mama' to her younger brothers and sisters. Her mother and father were working in the scorching sun from dawn to dusk, so there was no wonder she turned out to be one of the best cooks and homemakers, around.

I remembered her telling us about when her Daddy almost beat a man to death for asking him to let her habitually visit him to clean his house. She said something about him knowing the man was a nasty, old fart, and the thought of him trying to do something to his baby sent him into an "injun rage." Pop-Pop was half Cherokee Indian. *Wooo-weeee!* He could do some damage when he was enraged.

After that, they had to smuggle him out of town because they did not want him to go to jail. Big Mama said her mother believed it was better to have him giving money to them from another place than have him unable to provide any help for her and the children because of incarceration. I could somehow see that. She said this did not result in a good thing for Nana-T (her mother) because she missed him, terribly. She told us how Nana-T sneaked onto the porch and cried when she thought everyone slept. She said she walked to the yard's border and searched all directions for him...like she expected him to trudge from the fields. This never happened. He returned as a corpse being dumped upon the porch at midnight.

Nana-T did not know where he came from or who had left him there, but seeing his condition at that time did something awful to her mind. I hear tell he was so bruised and bloody; she could barely identify him. The occurrence frightened her so much; she insisted on having light until daybreak because she swore the darkness always revealed his face. Pop-Pop was a handsome man. He had wavy-black hair and green eyes. He worked and loved, fervently.

He never spanked Big Mama, her brothers, or sisters. One day, He admitted he could not bring himself to do it. Big Mama must have gotten her switch expertise from Nana-T because she had no problem breaking one out and getting busy. She would hit everything in her path without thinking about it, twice. I could just see her running, as a child, through the house and trying to hide as Nana-T raced through each room and looked for her.

Pop-Pop had been dumped on the porch. Several of the kids were older and capable of performing odd-and-end jobs to bring money, food, or clothes into the house. Nana-T kept busy by helping women deliver babies and washing extra laundry. One thing was certain, though; they could always tell when Pop-Pop's death bothered her.

They *knew* she was missing him whenever she conducted her roll call and had us sit on the porch with her. She could have sat on the porch and mourned for him, but she took advantage of the time to sew into us some of the stories that had been handed down to her by her parents. She would let them all bathe and get clean before coming out, so they would be clean in heaven if they died in their sleep like the other three. The nights she chose to tell them stories always seemed to agree with her.

The moon added an extra dose of serenity when it was full and shone, brightly. They would huddle up with their eyes all aglow and focus on her. Often times, mouths were wide open in disbelief from what they heard, and spirits were bubbling and unconfined when a story of triumph had been shared.

It was not long before I looked over and saw Daniel, Paul, Mary, and Justine were asleep. I could not go to sleep, though. There was something about how I had been awake and heard Big Mama sneaked out onto the porch that troubled me. I eased out of bed, went over, and made sure that they were fast asleep. I pushed arms and legs back onto the beds and pulled the covers up to their chins.

I waited until my eyes had adjusted to the darkness of the room and eased my way to Big Mama's room. I peeked in through the door, but she was not in bed. I sat there for a moment, listening in the quiet of the night. I heard the crickets singing their midnight sonatas, the cars passing in the night, and the house settling as the wind did a non-disturbing dance through it, but there were no signs of her.

I cocked my head to one side, and I heard a sound that was familiar in some ways and not the norm in others. I stretched my neck out a little farther, trying to navigate my way to it. It came from the porch. I tiptoed in that direction, and I could understand the sounds better as I got closer.

It was Big Mama; she was sitting on the porch crying. I turned to get back in the bed without hesitation, but I wanted to know what had saddened her.

"Come on out, chil'." My eyes got big, and I held my breath. She *knew* I was standing there. She called me out. I wanted to disappear, but she *knew* I was there. I had to go, now. I nervously set my feet in motion and stopped inside the screened doorway.

"Yes...yes, Big Mama?" She cleared her throat and tried to sound cheerful.

"What's wrong? Sum'n didn't sit well with ya' stumack?"

"No, Big Mama...I..I couldn't sleep, and I got up to use the rest room."

"Come on out here, chil'...you ain't gotta stand there like I'ma bite 'cha."

I quickly opened the screen door, walked over, and stood in front of her. I tried to get a feel for her mood.

"Big Mama?" She seemed to be staring at an imaginary spot on the porch when I called her name, but then she looked up at me.

"Yes Ruthie?...What is it baby?"

"Can...can you tell me about Big Daddy?"

She was silent for a minute, and I wondered if I had said the wrong thing.

"Chil,' why do you ask such nonsense?" Her tone was not harsh nor otherwise intimidating, so I took that as a sign that I had not messed up too bad.

"Well...you told us about Nana-T, and how she used to sit out on the porch and cry for Pop-Pop, and you told us how she used to tell y'all stories to get over it...and...and I've heard you out here crying before...and Big Mama...you tell us stories, too. I thought that if Nana-T did it, you have to be doing it for the same reasons."

She released a cackle that startled me at first, but then I chimed right on in with her. Then, the tears started, again. She reached out to me, and sat me right next to her, tears glistened in the dark of the night, and said, "Big Daddy, huh? You want to know about your Big Daddy...well, let's see...where can I start?"

She took the shawl from around her shoulders, and placed it over me as I curled up in her lap. She stroked my head, and the sonata of the crickets, the cars passing, and the house settling were the last things I heard before falling asleep in her lap...right there on the porch.

Humble Beginnings

The robust aroma of bacon cooking teased my nose and caused my mouth to water. It still managed to call my name and have my time of slumber cooperatively broken although I was asleep. In a few months, I would be going away to college, and the thought of not waking up to mom's hearty cooking was something that I refused to acknowledge. Saturdays and Sundays were spent with all of us: Mom, Dad, and we seven children. We sat together at the table, savoring our lives as well as the food.

My alarm clock had not gone off yet, and I wondered whether I should lie there a little longer or simply rise. It would be a full day, and I would probably be quite relieved to crawl back between the soft, fluffy coziness of this space I would soon vacate.

"Janelle?" Well, so much for that. It was Mom calling me from downstairs. I guess I had better get to moving and shaking, now.

"Good morning, Mother?" I replied, loudly.

"Morning Sweetie, I was calling to see if you were yet awake." "Yes. I am, and as soon as I shower and brush my teeth, I'll be right down."
What I heard next made me wonder.

"Oh! no rush! I only wanted to see how many 'early risers' there might be. Take your time dear."

I did not know if this was her way of teasing me, but it caused me to hurriedly get dressed and find my way downstairs where she was removing some biscuits from the oven. They looked to be a mile high, and the butter had caused them to be a rich, light brown. I closed my eyes and allowed myself to briefly drift, away.

The kitchen was inundated with the crisp and seductive blends of the bacon, biscuits, eggs, toast, and grits. I went to the silverware drawer and pulled out a knife. The butter was sitting on the table between the salt and pepper.

I carefully sliced each biscuit and slid a pat or two of butter upon them. I went and stirred the grits after this. I heard Malcolm, Kendra, and Jarrod scrambling about, so there would be full-blown activity occurring in a little while. Mom moved around so effortlessly; I sometimes found it hard to believe that she was nearing fifty. I only recalled she was forced into rest or otherwise being out of service after the others were born. She and Dad kept up with one another, very well. They often took evening strolls through the neighborhood or rode their bikes.

"Architect...a-r-c-h...architect...a-r-k…
….architect...a-r-c-h-i..." Timothy, who was in the third grade, was practicing his spelling bee words. The past few weeks had been spent with everyone listening to him go over the hundred words, which were listed on his sheet.

"Good morning, Mommy and Sissy." He went over, and gave mom a kiss on the cheek.

"Good morning, little man," I replied. "Good morning, Timmy. I heard you correct yourself a minute ago; that's always a good sign. You'll do a wonderful job sweetie." No one could have said it better than her. He made a rather snaggle-toothed smile and asked, "Mommy do you think I have a chance to win?" She stopped stirring the eggs, turned with her hands on her hips and said,

"Absolutely. With the way that you've been putting aside time to study and practice with all of us, I'd say that you have as good a chance as anyone." I cheerfully added, "Even if you don't win the spelling bee, you're still a champ in my book, kiddo." He blush a little when he ran into my arms.

"Sissy, I'm going to miss you when you go away to college. Will ya' write me?"
Mom looked proudly at me, and for a brief second, I got teary eyed. I had been so fortunate to be in a family like this. We had both of our parents, a beautiful home, a well-rounded and devoted cast of siblings, and a foundation that was indicative of a dedicated set of parents. I knelt upon my knees and ran my hand over his head.

"You just try to stop me. You'll be so sick of my letters that you'll tell the postman to stop delivering them." He kissed me on the nose and ran out of the kitchen. She stood there for a moment smiling at me. I walked over to her and put my arms around her waist while resting my head on her shoulder.

"What are you thinking Mrs. Adams? I haven't been your daughter for eighteen wonderful years, to not know when that beautiful mind of yours is working." She closed her eyes and squeezed me awfully hard.

"I'm just thinking of how lucky I've been to have you as my daughter, my friend, a second mother to the kids, and for the way that you've turned out. I'm so very proud of you and all of your accomplishments."

"Mother, everything that I am, you made me. Whatever pride you feel for me is ten-fold when it comes to my admiration of you. You've made a wonderful home for us. You're an outstanding wife to Dad and all of this without one ounce of regret. I could only hope to be able to nurture, provide for, and encourage my children as you have us.
Thank you." The rest of the gang made their presence known and interrupted our quiet moment. Jarrod and Timmy ran to their respective seats. Sonya and Tonya are 16-year old twins and the second oldest. They sat across from each other. They enjoyed the 'mirror effect' more than they revealed. Kendra and Malcolm strolled in with Dad.

"Good morning Adams clan." Uproars of "Good morning" echoed throughout the dining room. He walked over and kissed Mother on the forehead. They looked into one another's eyes and smiled a secretive smile. Something was up, and I could not wait to know.

"Architect...a-r-c-h-i...architect...a-r-t-i-...oops...I mean a-r-c-h-i-t-e..."

"Timmy, you can practice, more a little later? I don't want you to not have your food digest because you're so busy practicing those words. You'll do fine."

Dad had a very non-intimidating voice. He was a serious-looking man, but that meant nothing. He had eyes that seemed to look through you, but they only served to comfort and support you. He kept a neatly trimmed mustache. He was graying just above his ears, and one still might have estimated him to be a few years younger.

He ran track in high school and in college. Somehow, he managed to keep his physique within decent range over the years. He was a pharmacist at the county hospital. He loved the job and had shared how it intrigued him with us that he learned 0about drugs and healing things after reading a book of remedies, which were based on myths, old wives' tales, and superstition.

Mom had her Master's Degree in Marketing, but he told her he preferred for her to be a stay-at-home wife and mother after they married. She was more than happy to oblige. If she ever missed working, it was between her and the wind because we never had a reason to believe otherwise.

She was always wrapped into what we were doing and us. She was at nearly every practice, recital, or other extracurricular activity involving our participation. It was such a nice feeling to look up and see her clapping, cheering, or otherwise answering the call of motherhood. She received compliments all the time from women whom we would meet in passing. They were in complete awe of her having seven to handle, while they may have only had one or two.

We had a system, though. I was responsible for Jarrod who was thirteen. Sonya was responsible for eight-year-old Timmy. Tonya had the honor of keeping tabs on Malcolm, who was ten. Mom only had to worry about the baby girl, Kendra, who was four.

We were 'sibling pals.' This meant the older ones were responsible for seeing the younger ones were bathed, clothed, and did their chores. This allowed mom time to read, sew, and work in her garden or flowerbed. We thought we might be overwhelmed when Dad first approached us with the idea but there was nothing but smooth sailing after he explained how we would all benefit from it. The smaller ones were most cooperative and always made it a point to obey us.

This pairing off not only allowed us the opportunity to receive one-on-one attention from another family member, but it also afforded the entire family structure to be strengthened. I asked Mom and Dad to consider letting me go to community college, so I would still be closer and able to help them out more. They would not hear of it. Sonya and Tonya were rather mature and maternal, so they would step up to the plate and make it seem like I never left. Sonya liked to sing, and Tonya liked to write poetry.

They incorporated those gifts into their interactions with their charged siblings. Seeing Malcolm and Timmy sitting through their little talent shows and holding up cards in the end was funny. They showed the scores they had earned after an intense performance.

There was much wonder as to why they were not doing it professionally already since they always received '10s'. Clink...clink...clink! A sharp tapping on an orange juice glass broke me from my daydream.

"Can I have your attention please?" Everyone stopped what they were doing and looked over at Dad. He glanced over at Mom and smiled.

"I just wanted to share a bit of information with you children. Your mom and I have decided that it's about time for us to do something a little different for a change. We've all been rather busy with school, work, and the things that we do around here. So today, we'll be heading up to Lake Tranquility for a weekend of family relaxation. I'm very proud to say that as of yesterday, your mom and I made our last mortgage, and I feel that there would be no better way to breathe a sigh of relief than to enjoy one another during quiet time up there. We've arranged for a maid service to come in and clean the house today, so none of you have to worry about your chores."

Sonya and Tonya blew kisses to everyone and lipped "I love you" to Mom and Dad. The room became filled with screams of joy and celebration. Sonya and Tonya were discussing back and forth whether or not they wanted to let their friends know or just wait until Monday to tell them at school. Jarrod and Malcolm were already starting with the questions and wanting to be able to sleep outside on the porch. Kendra and Timmy did not seem to be interested one way or another, but they screamed and yelled, anyway. It probably seemed like the thing to do. Dad tapped the glass again to get our attention.

"With the lake being an hour and a half away, we'll need to go ahead and get situated, so that we can still enjoy it in the daylight hours, too."

Sonya interjected, "When will we be leaving Dad?" He put on a fake worried look and then shot a glance over to Mom.

"Hmmm...When would be a good time for us to leave dear?"

I knew there'd be no telling what was next when Mom put her hand to her cheek and pretended to have a deep thought working. She jumped up suddenly and shouted, "How about now?"

She and Dad raced out of the dining room as we sat there in disbelief. Mom forgot she had left Kendra, came back, swept her up in her arms and ran from the room. Tonya looked around at the rest of us and asked, "Umm...Why are we still sitting here?"

She barely got to finish before chairs were being pushed back from the table, bodies ran in every direction, and ruined the silence of the morning.

There was a traffic jam on the stairs, and we could hear Dad asking Mom what he should take as Timmy, Jarrod, and Malcolm ran from one room to the next and sought instructions with total chaos. Mom and Dad sat there looking at us as if they had been waiting around for hours by the time we had finished instructing the boys with their items and made our way to the den.

"Ken darling I don't know, we're both approaching fifty and yet we finished well before our wonderful children."

"Denise, sweetums, I think you're right. We could have been there and back by now. Couldn't we?" That was all he had to say.

Kendra yelled, "Last one to the car is a rotten egg!" The neighbors who were out washing their cars, mowing their lawns, or taking in the soft and gentle ambiance of the morning looked at us and shook their heads. Some were familiar with our hilarious antics, and some looked as if they really had concerns about our sanity. We loaded our bags into the car and did a roll call.

"Janelle and Jarrod are here."

"Sonya and Timmy are here."

"Tonya and Malcolm here."

"Kendra and mommy here." It was cute to hear Kendra's attempt at being a more independent and 'grown up' little person. Mom looked at her and winked her sign of approval.

We pulled out of the driveway and proceeded with the business of getting to the lake. Lake Tranquility was one of the most beautiful places you have ever wanted to visit. It had cabins that were chiseled into the mountainside, which overlooked the natural forestry on one side and had a breathtaking view of the lake on the other. The camping, fishing, and boating kept it occupied at different times of the year.

The nature trails took you through twists and turns, which gave the feel of well-organized rendezvous with the creatures occupying it. Busy squirrels scampered about and gathered nuts and berries. Birds swooped high and low and plucked worms and other, edible delicacies. Every now and then, a rustling of the brush would give you the opportunity to stare into the wide eyes of a deer.

We came to rest in front of the cabin that would be ours for the weekend after a few more turns. It whispered sentiments of past days. One could practically see the little, barefoot boys running around in pants being held onto them by a piece of rope or suspenders. I envisioned smaller girls sitting on the porch, pretending to have a tea party with imaginary friends.

If gently coerced, your mind could take you into the kitchen, where you could see the mother very carefully kneading the dough, which would be bread served with dinner. Turning slightly to your left or right would enable you to hear the powerful blows of the father, chopping firewood in the back.

"Daddy! Daddy! Can we go swimming now? Will you take us swimming?" Malcolm was excited, and he wanted to be able to show off the swimming skills Tonya had passed onto him.

"Sure son. Let's get everything in the house, and we can all come out and take a dip." The water was such a relief. It relaxed me and soothed my sun-drenched skin. Jarrod and I raced one another a couple of times, and I let him win. Mom and Dad took turns gliding Kendra through the water. She kicked her tiny little legs as if they were what had her making progress. Timmy and Malcolm were having a water fight. They had it going, everywhere. Without warning, it would turn into an all-out family affair.

Mom crept over and splashed water on Tonya, who in turn, splashed it on Sonya. Dad made it a point to join in on the free for all. Arms and elbows were all over the place. Needless to say, we went dragging into the house extremely exhausted and ready for bed. After bathing, we piled into the den to watch movies. I do not know how many we had watched them before they were all asleep.

I did not bother waking any of them. I pulled out extra blankets and covered them where they lay. I looked outside and saw Mom and Dad were still sitting at the edge of the lake talking as they enjoyed one another. I smiled and took my very tired self into the room and called it a night.

"Denise, I could never tell you what being married to you has meant to me. You've given me seven beautiful children, a loving home to come to after work, and support that can never be matched. I see you in them, each and every day, and every day, I thank God that HE saw fit to bring you to me." She suddenly turned away from the water and quietly wonders what brought this on.

"Ken, is there something that I need to know? Is there any particular reason that you are saying this?" He stood up and pulled her up to meet his embrace.

"No baby, there is no particular reason, but I don't know that I tell you enough. We see and hear about couples breaking up, every single day. We hear about how uncontrollable and defiant children are, but you have been the difference in why life for me and our children has been so worthwhile, and I love you for it."

They gently kiss, and she ran her fingers across his lips.

"Shh. You owe me no great accolades. Anything that I've been able to do has been because you have made it so. You have sacrificed much, so that our children could have me at home when they leave for school and when they come home. You have made it possible for me to have a warm dinner ready for our family when they make it in. Ken you've done all of that without once making me feel that I was of no help to you. The long hours at work, taking on a part-time job, and then refusing to have Janelle go to community college, even though it would save a substantial amount of money; that's extreme sacrifice. I wouldn't dare take that from you. I'll share it, but I'd never take it without your being allowed to shine."

"You are everything to me, and I needed you to know that. I wanted us to have this special vacation together because after Janelle leaves, Sonya and Tonya will be a few years later and so on and so on and so on. I felt it would be time better served while we were still under one roof. I wanted it to be one of the first things we'd remember when having an occasion to do so." Denise smiled and said, "Baby, you've given us all something we could never forget, not just today, but every day, and I love you because of it."

They slowly walked into the house. Crickets were chirping, owls were inquiring, and the moon was shining brightly over the tranquil waters of the lake, were phenomenal.

"Rise and shine! Rise and shine!" Jarrod was walking through the cabin and knocking on the doors at mother's request. Sleepy heads started moving around and preparing for the ride home. If we could get dressed and be in the car within the next thirty to forty-five minutes, we would be able to make it to church on time. It did not matter about the drive back home, Mom and Dad did not play about church, and we were going.

One by one, we stumbled out of bed and gathered up our belongings. Mom had made toast and put the eggs and bacon on it, so we had all of it rolled into one. We wiped our faces and hands and photographed a few pictures with the camera Aunt Lisa had given me for Christmas. Getting back home seemed to take less time than going. I guess this was usually the case. I listened to the chatter from everyone in the car and smiled inside because I knew it would become foreign to me.

I do not know if mother was going to crown Jarrod sibling pal of someone or not, but he had certainly matured over the past few months. Malcolm and Timmy were captivated with him, and they loved it when he asked them if they wanted to play ball with him. They were little men in little boys' bodies, and anything leading them to believe they were perceived as such was quite all right with them.

We pulled into the parking lot at church and groomed ourselves to enter. We received the usual smiles and greetings (as we went to "our" row). It started out as a joke at first, but now we really do have a pew, which was specifically for us. Mom and Dad always liked for us to sit together as a family, and it eventually pushed others to different seats as we grew. The pastor decided that this pew would be ours and proclaimed that we had 'earned' it.

Dad did not want Mom doing any extra work, so we dined outside of home after service. We found a table first, and we fixed the younger children's plates as Mom sat with them. We noticed how the other patrons were watching our every move, but we ignored them since we were accustomed to it. We bowed our heads and said "grace" after we were finished settling.

Clink...clink...clink...everyone stopped in the middle of a bite. That 'clinking' seemed to be a sign we were in for good news, but this time would catch us all a bit bewildered. We could not imagine what else there might be. It was not Dad who had done the tapping, though: it was Mom.

"Okay, I have a little announcement that I'd like to make now." This time, you could tell it was genuine when Dad looked surprised. I was trying to determine the nature of the announcement. Was she going to go back to school? Was she going to open a flower shop? What? I tried to study her expression like it would really help. She cleared her throat.

"I just wanted to say that all of you have made me very proud that I'm your mother. The sacrifices that you've made, and the constant giving, giving, and giving have made us what we are. I'd also like to take this time to tell you that in a few months...we'll be doing it all over, again." Dad's mouth fell open, and he sat there speechless for a few minutes.

We were giggling and throwing all kinds of questions at Mom. She kept looking at Dad who finally stood, went over to her side of the table, and planted a big wet one on her.

"I'm going to be a Dad, again. I'm going to be a Dad, again. Wow! Wow!" He turned and faced other customers, who were within earshot, stretched his hands out in front of him and said, "I'm going to be a Dad again!"

Sporadic clapping and whistling invaded the restaurant until Dad took his seat. I looked over at him and asked, "You sure I can't stick around and go to community college?" He shook his head and began to eat. I stole a glance over at Mom and mouthed the same thing to her. She shook her head and motioned for me to eat, but I could not start.

Instead, I reflected on how she had managed to do it with one and then kept on until we reached seven, and then tonight she's selflessly willing to do it, again. What made this even more fascinating to me was the fact Dad was as happy about this one as he was all the others.

I looked up and saw Kendra staring at me, intensely. I put my fork down and asked her, "What's wrong baby girl?" She put her hands to her face, shook her head, and asked, "Another baby? Oh brother! Can I go to school with you?" The restaurant erupted with cackling and astonished laughter from all whom had been privy to our conversation.

Strange Bedfellows

A balding, middle-aged man stood in the doorway of a room. He carefully observed the huddled mass of a man who was sprawled across the bed in nothing more than a tie and boxers. He quickly scanned the room and locked his sight on articles of a woman's clothing. He walked over for further inspection. There were panties and a lace slip. He hurried into the kitchen and retrieved a trash bag. He went throughout the rooms picking up and discarding items that he found as a regular routine, stealthily.

Take-out cartons from a nearby Chinese restaurant sat on the table along with long-stemmed wine glasses, which were half empty. He took his hand and swept everything into the bag.

He went into the restroom and snatched the used towels and washrags from the holders. He emptied the small wastebasket into the bag as well. In the living room he straightened the couch, fluffed the pillows, and emptied the ashtrays. He turned around, gave the place a thorough scan, and proceeded to the bedroom.

He stood and waited for signs of life, but none were revealed. He reached into his pocket and carefully eased over the man lying there without disturbing him. He took his hand out of his pocket, walked over, and gathered clothes that were thrown across a chair.

"Mr. President! Mr. President! Sir, we need to get going. A reporter from WRJT called your office, wishing to get confirmation of a story that you were having an extra-marital affair and would be here tonight. Sir, we need to get going before any overzealous gossip hounds infiltrate the place."

There was no answer, only slight movement. The gentleman became somewhat more frustrated and exclaimed, "Sir! We must leave at once. Reporters are on the way. I've already cleaned up and have a car waiting at the side entrance. With all due respect sir, I need you to move your ass! You're the President of the United States, and this would not be a good thing!" He scurried over and began to dress the less-than-sober man.

"What the hell are you doing? Leave me alone damn it!"

"Mr. President! I have covered for you since you became Commander-In-Chief, and I refuse to be a party to what the papers would do with a story like this. I beg you, sir. Please, get up and let's make our way from here." The President drowsily began to sit up. He mumbled and grumbled inaudibly, and asked a question:

"Sebastian, where is the woman? Where did she go?" This was hardly the time for him to be interested in the whereabouts of a cocaine-snorting hooker, but Sebastian satisfied his curiosity, anyway.

"She's gone sir. She left nearly an hour ago. You got a little sloppy this time. I did not see any condom wrappers in either of the wastebaskets. You can't afford another..." his voice trailed off, and the President turned to face him.

"You get great joy in rubbing my face in that mistake don't you? I bet you look forward to times that I've upset you, so you can throw my son up in my face! Don't you? Answer me!" Sebastian tossed the President his clothes and sharply answered, "Sir! Had I any desire to see you scorned and ridiculed, I would not have kept him, your drug use, or the cavorting with hookers hidden, all these years. Give me credit for something, sir." He stormed out and waited for the President to get dressed and join him.

The President groggily walked out and looked around the room. "You got everything?" Without looking at him Sebastian replied, "Yes sir, I did. It's imperative that we be on our way out. Please, sit now, so that I can disguise you." The President walked over and sat in the chair nearest the door. Sebastian opened a duffel bag and pulled out a man's wig and fake mustache. He carefully placed them on the President, and they walked briskly to the door. He held his hand up for the President to stop before he peeked out of the door.

"Clear, let's move, sir." Both men bowed their heads slightly and walked through the corridor with swiftness. Men in dark suits, scanning the perimeters, were obviously the President's Secret Service agents. They climbed into the car, and it sped off into the night, passing a WRJT news van, which turned into the hotel.

"Sebastian, I have to ask your forgiveness for the things that I said to you back there. You've been more than a dedicated assistant. You've been a lifesaver and a friend. Please, accept my apology as I mean it."

Sebastian did not answer, immediately. He sat wondering why a man, who had so much to lose, was willing to throw it all, away. He had three beautiful children and a gorgeous wife, yet they were not enough. He also had a six-year-old son, who was the result of an extra-marital affair. This was dangerous enough without adding a group of call girls, which he was on a first name basis with, and his hunger for cocaine and ecstasy.

The President still did not seem to be concerned about what it could cost him if any of this were revealed although he brought much honor and prestige to the Fifth Street Baptist Church and congregation. No one could argue the reasons that Sebastian had finally made the decision to walk away from it all.

"Sir, I can accept this apology as I have all the others, but sir, I have to inform you that at the end of this term....I will be tendering my resignation. I can't do this, anymore. I can't watch you self-destruct. The day could come when I'm not able to clean up a mess by passing another envelope of 'hush money' or by being a 'gone fishing' alibi for you, and I simply don't want to risk all that I've tried to accomplish as a result. You do understand, don't you sir?"

The phone rang. He answered it, and gave it to the President. "It's the First Lady, sir." He looked away as the President started his conversation with his wife.

"Yes darling. I'm fine. Sebastian and I are having a wonderful time. We wrapped up the talk with the administrators here, and I'll be back in Washington by noon, tomorrow. Yes dear I shall. Kiss the children for me and tell them that I love them." He hung up and looked over at Sebastian.

"Now, back to you and what you were telling me, Seb. I don't want to go at it without you. I know that I can be a stubborn jackass at times, but I wouldn't care to have anyone else in my corner. You've got to know what you've meant to me."

"Sir, how long do you think this charade will be able to play out? How long do you believe it'll be before some opponent, hell bent on destroying you, finds out that you are leading a less-than-fair life in and out of the White House? I'm telling you this because you're a good man, and I know that you have a good heart, but you have got to get a grip. You simply cannot afford a scandal of any magnitude." The President leaned forward and lowered his voice.

"Are you telling me this as my assistant or as my brother?" Sebastian shot him a troubled look and blazed back, "Sir! That is information that you should not be carelessly throwing around in the back of the car. It has nothing to do with our having the same father. You still cannot afford for anything negative to come along, and I simply cannot stand back and wait for it to happen."

The President buried his head in his hands and whispered, "Is there nothing that I can do to get you to change your mind?"

Sebastian sighed heavily before he responded, "Yes sir, there is something that you can do. It's more a matter of whether you're willing to do it." The President lifted his head.

"What is it you ask of me?" In a hushed tone, Sebastian replied, "Sir, as your brother AND your assistant, I ask that you rid yourself of these demons and salvage your good name, your honor, and the office of the Presidency. Consider all of the people who look up to and admire you. Are they not worthy of the best damned man possible heading this country?"

"Seb, you make it seem like I am out of control. You act as though I'm..." he cut his words short when he saw Sebastian had taken on a defiant and unwavering posture.

"Then, my intentions to resign at the end of this term stand. I'll be sure to get that in a sealed envelope to you as soon as we've returned to Washington. Thank you, sir." The President slumped back into his seat and remained silent for the remainder of the ride.

Their return to the White House was met with happy, bouncing children who swamped him with hugs and kisses.

"My goodness! My goodness! I've only been gone a weekend, and it's like I've been gone for months."

"That's because any time away from you seems like an eternity." He swung around to find the First Lady had entered. She rushed into his arms and kissed him.

"I'm so glad you're back home, dear. I hope Sebastian took good care of you." She looked over at Sebastian, teasingly. Then, she walked over to hug him as well.

"Sebastian, you take such good care of him when you're away on your business trips, fishing expeditions, and state business. What would he ever do without you?" He laughed and said, "Let's hope *he* never has to find out," and shot the President an all-too-knowing look. The President bristled and returned his attention to the children who ran to check his luggage for the usual gifts upon his return. He walked out, "Sara, Zachary, Melanie? I bet I know where y'all are. What might you be in to?"

A certain "chill" seemed to take over with the President and Sebastian. It had been weeks since their return from their last trip, and their dealings were more or less forced, somewhat animated. Sebastian was in the middle of a meeting with other White House staff when his private line rings.

"Yes sir, I'll be right there." He turned to the staffers and explained, "I'm sorry, but there has been an emergency with the President, and we'll need to close out this meeting until further notice."

He grabbed his briefcase and rushed past secret service agents into the President's office.

"Sir, what is it that couldn't wait until I had finished my meeting?" The President had slumped in his chair with obvious signs he had been crying. This caught Sebastian off guard.

"My God sir, what is the matter? What has you distraught?" The President pointed to the newspaper. He picked it up and scanned the page for whatever had caused the President's response.

An article caught his eye. He dropped down heavily in a chair. "Who? Why? I mean how? I don't understand." He read the article again and shook his head.

"This can't be, not her. Sir, I'm so sorry. I don't know what to say. I know what she meant to you. I adored her...I...are you going to be okay, sir?" The President was silent. He just sat, staring blankly at the picture of a beautiful, black woman he held in his hand.

This same face was the one that accompanied the article about a woman who was strangled and left in a ditch.

"Sebastian, I loved her more than life itself. She had brought me so much happiness and completed my very existence. When life was kicking me down...," he faltered, briefly. Then, he continued, "It was she who kept me grounded and continued to give me hope, no matter what was going on. Who would do something like this to such a beautiful creature? Seb, if this country was really ready for it and I knew it could be pulled off, she would have been the nation's First Lady."

"You never got over her, did you? To hell with the Presidency and the thoughts of others! Why would you not do all in the name of love? At least then, you would be happy. I'm looking at a shell of a man. One who has let everyone else dictate to him what he should be doing with his life, and I don't like it. Answer me this, sir: how are you going to handle this? How are you going to say goodbye to her? How suspicious would it be for the President of the United States to attend, acknowledge, or otherwise pay homage to a single, gorgeous, black woman who didn't do anything that would have warranted his attention and who was also murdered?" The President stood and slammed his fists upon his desk.

"By God! I will not let her leave here without acknowledging her! I don't know how, but I do know that I will be with her, again...for the last time. Seb, she was the first woman I ever loved. She was the first woman to make me accountable for what I chose to do. She...she..." He fell back into his chair and buried his face in his hands and cried, uncontrollably. Sebastian went over to him and placed a hand on his shoulder.

"I'll take care of it, sir. I'll come up with something that'll make your presence less suspicious and your love for her more worthy of a presidential tribute. If I sounded insensitive, it was not my intent; it was the assistant side of me speaking, but now...and as your brother...I have to say that I loved her, too. I've always known what she meant to you, but it was your call as to how you would proceed with the relationship. Times like this are what make what I do hard. So many have to pay the price for the actions of others, and the guilty walk free."

He turned and moved toward the door. He reached to open it, and the President raised his head and asked, "What did you say I'd have to do to keep you here with me? I can't do it by myself Seb...I...I can't try to go it, alone. If I do it...it'll have to be with my knowing that I have a solid force backing me. I don't know anyone else who could do that for me, only a brother." Sebastian smiled, "I'll be sure to get in touch with him, and let him know that you'll be expecting him."

Beatrice Sleeps Forever

Once upon a time, there was a beautiful, Nubian Princess named Beatrice. She was the middle child of the King and the Queen of Sleepy Town. They were very gracious and loving rulers. They never imposed anything on the townspeople they would not endure themselves, but one thing they were very strict about was having the children in Sleepy Town taking naps before 3:00 p.m. or withstanding three nights without sleep.

One Sunday afternoon, Beatrice found she was unusually tired and wanted to sleep. It was well past the 3:00 time frame allotted, so she was in a tizzy. Much to her surprise, she found herself falling asleep while sitting in the berry patch, where she had been sent to gather them.

A gentle nudge would awaken her, and she was quite surprised to see the No Zee Zee After Three guards standing over her. She was led into the chambers of her parents, crying with a bowed head.

Her siblings were rushed out of the room and assured Beatrice would be alright. King Gotosleepontime cleared his throat and looked out at his daughter.

"My dear child, what have you to say for yourself?" Beatrice looked over at her mother who was distraught and unable to look at her, directly. Then, she redirected her attention to her father.

"I don't know what came over me, father. I was in the middle of gathering berries, and...and the strangest urge to go to sleep befell me."
She threw herself to his feet and wept. Her mother could not stand to see this and cried as she ran out of the room.

"Look what you've done to your mother. Have you no shame little one?" His thunderous voice rang throughout the room.

"Oh father! Yes, yes I am ashamed of this transgression against you, but it wasn't all my fault. I did try to fight it. I did get up and move around often, but in the end...I guess...I guess I wasn't as strong as you or mother would need me to be."

"My child, you know what the consequence of this crime will be. Have you anything to say before I pass sentence?" Beatrice looked at her father unbelieving and somewhat defiant, now.

"Yes father, I have something to say, I want to know if it would be *okay* for you to join me in my three nights of sleep deprivation, as I saw *you* asleep at 4:30 last evening, and I uttered not one word to the servants or to anyone. I kept it to myself. So, how about it? Will you be joining me, or will we take this to mean that I'm a lot more like you than we first realized?"

At this, the king clapped his hands together tightly and ordered that she be taken to the dungeon. He went to the door's opening and spoke with her after she was shackled to the walls and fed a light supper.

"Foolish child! Why would you put me in a position to have to do this to you?" She managed a weak smile and replied, "Dearest father, I am not long for this world. Something has taken a hold of me and has me sleeping more and more against my will. Rather than continue to shame you and put you in the position of having to punish me…I'd rather die once than have you die each and every time that you see me go through it."

In utter disbelief and great agony over this, he spoke to her in a loud whisper, "Have you gone mad? What words do you speak? Who has harmed your mind, child?" She said nothing, and she slumped to one side as he summoned guards to allow him entry as she faintly said, "It's the guards...one of the guards...he's poisoned me and this will be my farewell."

Beatrice sleeps forever, now...

Made in the USA
Middletown, DE
26 April 2019